HISTORICAL RECORDS

OF THE

1st KING'S OWN STAFFORD MILITIA,

NOW

3RD AND 4TH BATTALIONS

SOUTH STAFFORDSHIRE REGIMENT.

COMPILED BY

CAPTAIN C. H. WYLLY,

ADJUTANT 3rd BATT. SOUTH STAFF. REGT.,

TO 1892,

AND BY

COLONEL CHARRINGTON, C.M.G.,

AND

CAPTAIN BULWER,

ADJUTANT 4th SOUTH STAFF. REGT.,

TO 1902.

Lichfield:
A. C. LOMAX'S SUCCESSORS, THE "JOHNSON'S HEAD."
1902.

HISTORICAL RECORDS.

HISTORICAL RECORDS.

1st KING'S OWN STAFFORD MILITIA.

During the time of the great national troubles under King Charles I., the Royal Army was raised by the nobility and gentry, who adhered to the Royal Cause, from among their tenants and dependents, and the following extract from an Act of Parliament dated 2nd December, 1648, appoints Commissioners for the County of Stafford and the City of Lichfield, viz :—

Die Sabbathi, 2 Decemb. 1648.

An Ordinance for the setling the *Militia* in the several
Counties, Cities, and places within the Kingdom
of *England*, Dominion of *Wales*, and Towne
of *Barwick* upon *Tweed*.

THE Lords and Commons Assembled in Parliament, finding it necessary, That the severall Counties of the Kingdome of *England* and Dominion of *Wales*, and Towne of *Barwick*, be put into a Posture of Defence, for the preservation and safety of the King, Parliament, and Kingdome ; Do Ordaine, and be it hereby Ordained by the said Lords and Commons, That for the setling of the *Militia* in the Kingdome and Dominion aforesaid, and Towne of *Barwick*, The persons hereafter named, shall be Commissioners for the several Counties, Cities, and places for which they are hereby respectively appointed Commissioners : *Viz.*

For Staffordshire, and the City of Litchfield.

Sir *William Brereton, Iohn Bowyer, Thomas Crompton, Edward Lee, John Swinfen, Michael Noble, Samuel Terrick, William Jolly, Edward Broghton, Mathew Morton, John Chetwood, Henry Stone, George Bowes, Michael Biddulph, Philip Iackson, Roger Hurt,*

Richard Flyer, Iohn Young, Lester Barber, Joseph Whithovgh, Edward Manwaring.

Most of the Militia of the Country, and particularly the Trained Bands of London, sided with the Parliament. After the restoration of King Charles II., feudal tenures being abolished by Act of Parliament, a National Militia was established, and housekeepers and other substantial persons were bound to find men, horses, arms, ammunition, and pay, each according to their real or personal estates. This Militia was declared by Act of Parliament to be under the immediate orders of the King, but was seldom mustered owing to the great expense, and fell into abeyance. About the year 1756, the Nation being alarmed by apprehension of an invasion, the Militia was again instituted, and called out on service. On the capture of Quebec by General Wolfe in 1759, the war with France terminated, and the Militia were dispersed to their homes and remained disembodied until the year 1776. It would appear that a Stafford Militia was first raised in the year 1648, and consisted of a Regiment of Foot and two Troops of Horse, under the command of Colonel John Bowyer, of Knypersley. This force garrisoned the town of Leek, was most undoubtedly a County Militia, and was employed in the seizure of the Regicide, Major-General Harrison, as the following extract from " The History of the House of Stuart " proves :—

1648

Colonel Bowyer, without any order, took a party of the Staffordshire Militia, and by his own authority, seized Major-General Harrison with his horses and arms. The Major-General had notice that Bowyer would do so if he did not fly from it, which he absolutely refused, looking upon it as flying from the Cause, tho' in truth the Cause fled from him. But there was as much enthusiasm in his political, as in his religious, principles."

Major-General Harrison was executed in October, 1660.

During this year, in the war between Great Britain and **1776.** her American dependencies, the Staffordshire Militia was once more raised and embodied, and consisted of eight companies—28 sergeants, 18 drummers, and 560 rank and file. The following officers were appointed to the Regiment on its embodiment, viz. :—Colonel—the Right Hon. Lord Paget ; Lieut.-Colonel—Sir John Wrottesley, Bart. ; Major John Daniel ; Captains—Richard Whitworth, John Jervis, Hon. Charles Finch, Richard Taylor, and Walter Sneyd ; Captain and Lieutenant—William Carey ; Lieutenants—Bartholomew Reynolds, John Townsend Gollins, and Edward Kempson.

The following officers were added to the Regiment in 1778, viz. :—Captains—Richard Dyott, and Edward Disbrowe; Lieutenants—Bourne Fernyhough, Edmund South, William Handley, Nicholas Jackson, Charles Robinson, and David Buffington ; Ensigns—Charles Greenhead, George Reynolds ; Surgeon—Thomas Peake ; Surgeon's Mate—Charles Greenhead ; Chaplain—Edmund Elliott ; Adjutant—Bartholomew Reynolds ; Quarter-Master—Nicholas Jackson.

The Staffordshire Militia was, during this year, quartered **1778.** at Lichfield, but soon moved to Winchester, and was encamped there. Whilst there, the Regiment was augmented by a " Volunteer Company." It returned to Winter quarters at Lichfield in December.

The following extract from the " Gentleman's Magazine" of 1788 may be of interest.

The following anecdote regarding Serjeant Sarjant, of the Grenadier Company in the Staffordshire Militia, formerly of the Regulars, and which reflects so much honour on the character of a general officer, deserves to be recorded. As the Regiment was marching off the parade at Waterdown Camp to the field of exercise,

General Fraser, who was the Commander-in-chief, called out, " Step
out, old Serjeant." The Sergeant, who was uncommonly tall, being
apprehensive that by so doing he should throw the battalion-men
into disorder, though the Grenadiers might keep up with him, and,
piqued for the honour of the Regiment, which stood very high in the
scale of military estimation, ventured to destroy the command, by
pretending not to hear it ; upon which the General repeated it with
the addition of a menace, that if he did not step out, he would order
the men to tread upon his heels. The Serjeant, however, rather chose
to run the hazard of any consequences to himself from his perse-
verance, than of the least disgrace which might befall the Regiment.
The General, probably imagining his command would now be obeyed,
directed his observations elsewhere ; but the poor Serjeant was
extremely mortified at this public rebuke, and his chagrin appeared
so strongly marked in his countenance, that his Captain, who was
witness to the whole affair, mentioned it to the Earl of Uxbridge,
then Lord Paget, and Colonel of the Regiment, who, with the rest of
the officers was engaged to dine with the General that day, and who
gave him such a character of the Serjeant, as induced him to make him
a reparation as public as the rebuke had been. Accordingly, on the
day when the camp broke up, the Regiments being all drawn out, the
General called out to him, " Serjeant Sarjant ; " and when he came
up to him took a silver-mounted sabre from his belt, and said, " You
will accept of this, and wear it for my sake, as a token of the great
opinion I entertain of you as a soldier, and a non-commissioned
officer ; " and then, to enhance the value of the gift, turning to Lord
Paget, said, " This sabre is not agreeable to the Staffordshire uniform ;
and therefore, I beg your Lordship will give the old gentleman leave
to wear it whenever he pleases "; to which his Lordship assented. It
would be an act of injustice to his noble patron, not to mention, that
when he quitted the command of the Regiment soon after, he directed
the Serjeant to draw on him annually for twenty guineas. The sabre
and its scabbard were placed across each other on his coffin, at his
funeral, which was celebrated with the usual military honours. He
has bequeathed it to one of the brothers of his Captain, who is an
officer in America.

1779.　　In January of this year, six companies of the Regiment
were quartered at Lichfield, and three at Burton-on-Trent.
In February, five companies were sent to Stafford, and in July
the whole of the Regiment was quartered at Stafford.

On the 12th March, 1779, Lord Lewisham was appointed Lieut.-Colonel of the Staffordshire Militia, *vice* Lieut.-Colonel Sir John Wrottesley promoted into the Line.

In August the Regiment was again quartered at Lichfield, and in September marched to Bristol, leaving detachments at Andover, Basingstoke, Overton, and Whitchurch.

During this year, the Staffordshire Militia was quarter- 1780. ed at Southampton, Winchester, and Waterdown, moving into Winter quarters at Liverpool in October.

The Regiment marched to Scarborough in May, and 1781. remained there till October, when it returned to Lichfield. Lord Lewisham was appointed Colonel *vice* Lord Paget resigned.

In January the Staffordshire Militia was quartered at 1782. Lichfield, Newcastle, Stafford, Stone, Rugeley, and Penkridge. It was ordered to proceed to Warley Camp, Essex, in June, and under command of Lord Lewisham was reviewed by General Lord Townsend in November, and then marched to, and was quartered at, Leighton Buzzard, Amersham, and Windover.

In March, the Regiment received orders to march to 1783. Staffordshire, and on its arrival at Lichfield was disembodied, having been embodied for seven years. In this year Lord Lewisham resigned, and Lord Uxbridge, formerly Lord Paget, was again appointed colonel. It is of the latter nobleman that Shaw, in his " History of Staffordshire," writes :—

Great praise is due to the Earl of Uxbridge for his unparalleled services to his King and Country, both military and naval, not only in his own personal exertions as Colonel of the Staffordshire Militia (which both for discipline and splendour have long been unrivalled), but likewise in training most of his sons to similar services.

The following is a list of the officers present with the Regiment at its disembodiment in 1783 :—Colonel—Lord Lewisham ; Lieutenant-Colonel—Asheton Curzon ; Major— W. Sneyd ; Captains—R. Whitworth, R. Dyott, E. Disbrowe, W. Carey, T. Mountford, and F. Heming ; Captain and Lieutenant—J. W. Winter ; Lieutenant and Adjutant—B. Reynolds ; Lieutenants—T. Gollins, B. Fernyhough, E. South, W. Handley, C. Robinson, D. Buffington, R. G. Hand, A. Fitzgerald, and J. White ; Ensigns—G. Reynolds, C. Walker, F. Carey, J. Handsward, W. Adlam, and J. Altery ; Surgeon—J. Peake ; Surgeon's Mate—C. Walker ; Quartermaster—C. Robinson.

The Staffordshire Militia was trained twice during the ten following years of peace. In the first training Captain Carey acted as adjutant, and in the second training, Captain Miller acted in that capacity.

1793. War with France having been declared in this year, the Staffordshire Militia was once more embodied for actual service. The following officers were present at the time of its embodiment, viz. :—Colonel—The Right Hon. the Earl of Uxbridge ; Lieutenant-Colonel—W. Sneyd ; Major—E. Disbrowe ; Captains—T. Mountford, F. Heming, The Right Hon. Lord Paget, The Right Hon. Lord Gower, The Hon. W. Bagot, and J. W. Winter ; Captain and Lieutenant— The Right Hon. The Earl of Belfast ; Lieutenants—R. G. Hand, J. Neale, T. T. Gollins, E. South, H. Miller (Adjutant), Hon. A. Paget, A. B. St. Leger, J. Dyott, J. W. Greene, G. R. H. Reynolds, T. Fernyhough, and R. Gildart ; Ensigns—L. Y. Darwell, E. H. Mainwaring, L. G. Reynolds, F. Darwell, and G. Heming ; Surgeon—J. W. Greene ; Surgeon's Mate—F. Darwell ; Quarter-Master—B. Reynolds. The Right Hon. Lord Gower was afterwards appointed Colonel to the 2nd Staffordshire Militia when it was raised in 1798.

In 1793 the Staffordshire Militia marched to Devonshire, and was finally quartered at Plymouth. It was here instructed in the New Regulations laid down by General Sir David Dundas, by Lieutenant Dyott (afterwards Colonel of the 63rd Foot), and under that officer's instructions gained considerable celebrity.

The Regiment was quartered at Weymouth during these 1794. two years, and was frequently reviewed by H.M. King George 1795. III.

Previous to its departure from Weymouth, the following Regimental order was published :

Lord Uxbridge desires to express in the strongest terms the great satisfaction he has received from the conduct of the Regiment during the campaign. He feels himself particularly obliged to the officers for their attention, and to the non-commissioned officers and men for their orderly behaviour. The skill and attention of Doctor Northen to the sick has met with the highest praise from Doctor Morris and Mr. Keate, the Inspector General of Military Hospitals.

On the 22nd September, 1796, the Staffordshire Militia marched to Shrewsbury in two divisions, and was billeted there.

In November, a detachment, consisting of 4 sergeants, 4 corporals, 2 drummers, 1 fifer, and 96 rank and file, under Captain Metcalf, was sent to Wenlock to quell riots.

In this year the Regiment was stationed at Liverpool, 1797. Dorchester, Weymouth, and Winchester, and was frequently inspected by H.M. King George III., who was so pleased with the fine appearance and high character of the corps that he soon after signified his pleasure that the Staffordshire Militia should be sent to Windsor to take the Royal duties.

In this year an Act was passed to augment the Militia, and a considerable addition was made in the County of Stafford of upwards of 2,000 men. These were called the "Staffordshire Supplementary Militia," and were called out and drilled under command of Lieutenant-Colonel W. C. Madan. In February, 1798, this Supplementary Militia was embodied at Lichfield, and was then formed into the 2nd and 3rd Staffordshire Militia.

1796. The 1st Staffordshire Militia (for there were now three Regiments of Staffordshire Militia (received its route for Windsor on the 10th June, and marched to that place from Winchester. On its arrival at Windsor the following order was published by Lieutenant-Colonel Sneyd, who appears to have brought the Regiment to a high state of discipline and efficiency.

Windsor, 14th June, 1798.—Parole "Staffordshire."—His Majesty having been pleased to make choice of the Staffordshire Regiment to do the Windsor duty this Summer, the Colonel wishes to observe to the men how necessary it is to appear as a Regiment ought to do, which is particularly selected to be near the person of the King.

1799. In the summer of this year, a general volunteering took place from the Militia to the Line. Lord Gower obtained permission, as Colonel of the 2nd Staffordshire Militia, then quartered at Winchester, to raise a Regiment for foreign service from the three Regiments of Staffordshire Militia. Three hundred men were soon formed from these Regiments, but owing to some objections offered by His Majesty, the scheme fell through, and the men were discharged. The men remaining of the 2nd and 3rd Regiments, were incorporated with the 1st Regiment of Staffordshire Militia on the King's duty at Windsor.

At the beginning of the year, the 1st Staffordshire 1800. Militia returned to Lichfield, to Winter quarters. In May, however, a route was received for the Regiment to return to Windsor for duty. It arrived in June, in time for His Majesty's birthday parade. King George III. received the Regiment on its arrival, most graciously greeting the officers who had the honour to be known to him. At a fête given at Frogmore, this year, by His Majesty, the Regiment furnished a guard of honour under command of Captain Gildart, with Lieutenant Hand and Ensign Colt, and the men of the Regiment took part in the entertainment, with singing, acting, &c.

In the summer of this year, the Regiment moved to 1801. Weymouth, and remained there till October, when it returned to Windsor. After the ratification this year of the Peace of Amiens, the whole of the British Militia were disembodied. When the 1st Staffordshire Militia left Windsor, King George III. accompanied it for about two miles, and expressed his regret at its departure in a manner highly gratifying and flattering to the Regiment.

The Corps arrived at Stafford in three divisions, on the 26th April, and was disembodied, after a continuous service of nine years. On its arrival at Stafford it was met by crowds of people, and was greeted with ringing of bells and general congratulations. The soldiers, on the day of their arrival, delivered over their arms, which they had carried so long with honour to themselves and to their County.

1803. The peace was of short duration, and the War with France again broke out early this year, and on the 30th March an order to embody the 1st Regiment of Staffordshire Militia was issued by the Lord Lieutenant of the County, and on the 17th May a route from the War Office was received by express, ordering the Regiment to return immediately to Windsor to resume the Royal duties. King George III. met the Regiment on its arrival, and placing himself at its head preceded it to Windsor Barracks. The Regiment was greeted with the utmost enthusiasm by the inhabitants of the Royal Borough. Major Disbrowe was appointed Vice-Chamberlain to H.M. Queen Charlotte.

The following is a roll of the officers who were present at the embodiment of the Regiment this year :—Colonel—The Earl of Uxbridge ; Lieut.-Colonel Sneyd ; Majors—Disbrowe, and F. Newdigate ; Captains—Heming, Wormsley, Simpson, Wolseley, Palmer, Swiney, Neale, Phillips, Coyney, Newton, Armstrong, and Wrottesley ; Lieutenants—Miller, Hand, Northern, Horton, Vallance, Whieldon, Hallen, Edwards, Wilkinson, Colt, Every, Ferneyhough, Jordan, and Stephens ; Ensigns—Riddlesdon, Mellor, and Bennett ; Adjutant—C. Wilkinson ; Quartermaster—W. Horton ; Surgeon—G. Wood ; Paymaster—H. Miller.

1804. It this year the Regiment moved to Weymouth and was reviewed there by King George III., who was accompanied by the Dukes of York, Sussex, and Cambridge. His Majesty expressed much pleasure and gratification at the manœuvres and the discipline of the Regiment. On its return to Windsor in November, the 1st Staffordshire Militia was again reviewed by King George III. in the Little Park. The King was much pleased with the fine appearance of the

Regiment, and expressed his high appreciation of its discipline, and was most graciously pleased to exclaim, " They shall be called my own ! " In consequence of these words of approval from His Majesty, the following order was issued by the Earl of Uxbridge, announcing the distinction conferred by the King on the 1st Staffordshire Militia :—

R.O.—Parole.—King George. WINDSOR,
21st May, 1805. **1805.**

Lord Uxbridge has received His Majesty's command to express to the 1st Staffordshire Militia his entire approbation, not only from its steady appearance in the Field this day, but also from its general good conduct during the time it has been under his own eye, and His Majesty has been graciously pleased, in reward for its merit, to confer on the Regiment the high honour of being in future named " The King's Own Stafford Militia."

Up to this date the uniform of the Regiment had been scarlet with yellow facings and silver lace, which was now changed to scarlet with blue facings and Staff collar, and the epaulettes gold, and the officers were entitled to wear the device of " Windsor Castle " on their accoutrements. His Majesty was graciously pleased to present some glass decanters to the officers' mess. These decanters are still in use, and are much prized by the officers of the Regiment.

Lieut.-Colonel Sneyd, " The Father of the Regiment," retired from the Service in April 1805, to the great and universal regret of the whole Regiment, and was succeeded as Lieut.-Colonel by Major F. Newdigate.

The 1st King's Own Stafford Militia went to Portsmouth in the summer of this year, but soon returned to Windsor.

In this year the Regiment gave a large and most mag- **1806.** nificent ball at Windsor. Over 500 invitations were issued.

His Majesty King George III. was present at the entertainment, and at the top of the room was placed an immense " Stafford Knot" in variegated lamps.

1809. 398 men, and a number of officers, volunteered from the Regiment to the Line.

1812. In this year the Earl of Uxbridge died, and was succeeded by Major the Earl of Dartmouth, who was appointed Colonel. Major Disbrowe, too, retired this year, after 34 years' service in the Regiment.

On the 21st April, orders were received for the 1st King's Own Stafford Militia to leave Windsor and to proceed to Chelmsford and Colchester. Before its departure the Mayor and Corporation of Windsor presented an address to the Regiment, extolling their soldier-like qualities and orderly conduct. The following order was published by Lieut.-Colonel F. Newdigate :—

WINDSOR,
22nd April, 1812.

The very flattering and distinguished manner in which the inhabitants of Windsor have taken leave of the Regiment is an honourable proof of the general good conduct of both officers and men during the long period of their stay at Windsor.

Lieut.-Colonel Newdigate can add no praise of his own to such a flattering testimony ; he participates in the pride which the Regiment must naturally feel in possessing a so deservedly high character, and is confident wherever the Regiment may serve in future, it will continue to maintain the high reputation of the King's Own Stafford.

The following letter, dated 27th April, 1812, was received from Horse Guards :—

SIR,—The Commander-in-Chief has received the Queen's commands to convey to you, and through your means to the Officers, Non-Commissioned Officers, and Men, cf the Regiment under your command,

Her Majesty's most gracious approval of their conduct during the period they have been stationed at Windsor.

The Commander-in-Chief is persuaded that the Regiment will be highly gratified by this intimation, and His Royal Highness has been desired further to inform you that every branch of the Royal Family, resident at Windsor, unites in these most gracious sentiments expressed by Her Majesty.

The Commander-in-Chief adds his tribute of applause as to the orderly and soldier-like manner in which the Regiment has performed its duties, which, he is assured, has conciliated the regard, and obtained for them the general respect and esteem of the Inhabitants of the Town and neighbourhood of Windsor.

I have the honour to be, Sir,

Your most obedient humble servant,

HARRY CALVERT,

Adjutant-General.

On the 21st November, the 1st King's Own Stafford 1813. Militia was summoned to London from Colchester, with 60 rounds of ball ammunition, and relieved the Foot Guards at St. James's and Kew Palaces.

On the Peace of Paris, the Regiment received a route to 1814. march to its County, and to be disembodied. It proceeded in three divisions, and was received by the inhabitants of Staffordshire with every demonstration of joy, it having been absent from the County for eleven years.

The Regiment remained disembodied till the escape of 1815. Buonaparte from Elba, when it was once more embodied, and marched to Derby and Nottingham, where it remained till April, 1816, when it once more returned to its County, and the men were dismissed to their homes.

The following extracts from orders issued from time to time in the old 1st King's Own Stafford Militia may be of interest as showing the regulations for dress, discipline, and interior economy in force in those days.

10th April, 1797. Morning Regimental Order.

In consideration of the Regiment having now two good suits of cloathes, Lieut.-Colonel Sneyd thinks it will be much to their advantage to receive the following articles instead of the cloathing that will be due to them at Midsummer next, viz. :—

Two pair of blue cloth pantaloons. One waist coat. Two pair of short black cloth gaiters. One exceeding good black leather cap and tuft. A black leather stock and rozette for the hair. A foraging cap, and half-a-guinea allowance in money to be paid when the cloathing money for the year 1797 is paid by Government.

If they are of the same opinion, he desires they will immediately signify it to him thro' the Officers Commanding Companies, in order that if the Colonel consents to the exchange, the things may be ordered as soon as possible.

14th June, 1797. R.O.

Officers are requested to provide themselves with blue pantaloons and short boots. Gorget strings to be the colour of the facings of the Regiment, agreeable to the King's Order.

30th June, 1797. R.O.

" The Regiment to parade to-morrow morning at seven o'clock in their old cloaths and caps. The Grenadiers and Light Infantry and Drummers in their respective dress caps. Musick in jackets. The Blacks in their best turbans. The Town Guard to-morrow will be furnished by the Battalion Companies whose new cloathing is fitted, the men for this guard will have their new hats properly fitted with strings, etc.

Negroes appear to have been employed in the band for beating the cymbals and triangles. The big drummer was also a negro.

The following order shows the power of the Commanding Officer.

30th July, 1797. R.O.

Sergeant Joseph Marsh of the Major's Company is suspended from rank and pay for fourteen days, by order of the Commanding Officer, and is to do duty and receive pay as a Private Soldier for that time.

1st December, 1797. R.O.

The Orderly Non-Commissioned Officers of each Company must be particularly careful that the men do not comb their hair or clean their shoes in the sleeping rooms, as the Commanding Officer is determined to make them answerable for the cleanliness of them.

This order was presumably on account of the powder from the men's hair flying about and settling in the rooms.

5th May, 1800. R.O.

The Sergeants will parade the men from the Second and Third Regiments every day after dinner and practice them to pass and salute an Officer, this must be done in a smart and soldier-like manner.

This order was published after the Supplementary Staffordshire Militia was incorporated for duty at Windsor with the 1st Staffordshire Militia.

23rd October, 1800. R.O.

The Regiment to parade to-morrow morning in review order at quarter after nine o'clock, in the highest order possible.

From the steadiness and attention of the Regiment for some time past the Commanding Officer has no apprehension respecting their appearance and performance to-morrow, and has no doubt but that they will again deservedly obtain the approbation and commendation of His Majesty, he feels convinced that any exhortations from him either to officers or men are perfectly unnecessary ; he requests that the officers will be particularly attentive to an exact uniformity in dress, and as there may be some not acquainted with what is exactly correct, for their information he mentions for Mounted Officers, leather breeches ; for all others kersymere, or cloth with quears, and feathers, as in the orders of yesterday.

From the following order it would appear that the officers' attendance on parade was not all that could be desired.

2nd November, 1803. R.O.

The Commanding Officer is sorry to be under the necessity of reminding the officers that their attendance on Parade is a duty which cannot be dispensed with. Every officer not having leave to be absent, is expected to attend the morning Parades ; and in the evening when they are prevented attending by other engagements, they are desired to leave their names and reason of absence upon a slip of paper in the Orderly Room, which paper the Adjutant will give to the Officer Commanding the Parade.

The Annual Musketry Course would appear to have been a very simple one, the distance fired at short, and the prizes given somewhat small, by the following order.

26th February, 1804. R.O.

On Monday next the Regiment will commence firing by Companies at the target by single shots, a Company each day, and two shots each man, 100 paces distant. Premiums will be given to each Company as follows :—

The best shot	7	shillings.
2nd ,, ,, ...	5	,,
3rd ,, ,, ...	4	,,
4th ,, ,, ...	2	,,
5th ,, ,, ...	1	,,

The tailors, batmen, cooks and Pioneers, will fire with their respective Companies.

The Commanding Officer of each Company will give a return to the Commanding Officer of the Regiment of the *names of such men as hit the Target*, marking those who will be entitled to prizes.

No other person to fire at the Target but corporals and privates, and particular care to be taken that each man fires out of his own firelock.

The soldier of olden days was evidently as fond of keeping dogs and pets in the Barrack Room as his successor of the present day, according to the following order.

7th August, 1804. R.O.

The number of dogs in Barracks having now become a nuisance, the Commanding Officer is obliged to insist on the Barrack Regulations, that no dog is to be admitted into the Barracks, be strictly enforced, and after Thursday morning every dog found within the surrounding wall of the Barrack Yard is to be hanged by the pioneers. Officers who have dogs that they value, will, between this and that period, take the necessary steps that they are kept in proper places so that they may not incommode their brother officers who do not keep dogs.

Swearing, and the use of profane language, seems to
have been much in vogue amongst the Staffordshire soldiers
of that day, and it appears to have been necessary to take
steps to prevent it.

2nd September, 1804. R.O.

Lieut.-Colonel Sneyd has been much shocked since he has
lived in camp by the expressive and constant habit of swearing he
has observed amongst the soldiers.

A habit wicked in its effect and disgraceful to those who practice
it.

He is determined as far as he is able to prevent their foolish
vice, and desires that every officer, and non-commissioned officer,
who shall hear any man of his Company swearing after this notice, will,
for the first offence, give him a proper reprimand ; for the second,
order him a duty of fatigue; for the third, an additional guard ; and
after that confine him and report him to the Commanding Officer.

Three oaths was apparently the limit allowed to each
soldier. This would seem but a moderate allowance to the
soldier of the present day !

23rd January, 1805. R.O.

Any woman seen in the streets with the great coat on belonging to her husband will be immediately turned out of the Barracks,
and her husband punished.

An extraordinary, but, no doubt, a very necessary
order !

3rd May, 1806. R.O.

The price of the men's washing to be throughout the
Regiment at fivepence a week from each man, to be paid to the
woman by the Pay Sergeants ; and may be stopped from those men
out of debt from their monthly stoppages, but from those in debt
it must be stopped from their week's subsistence.

What would Tommy Atkins say now-a-days to fivepence
a week for washing ?

27th December, 1806. R.O.

The men confined to Barracks being frequently seen in the
streets, and one having deserted last night, the Sergeant of the

Guard is to call the roll of them three times from the evening parade until the taptoo rolls are called. A fifer will attend at the guard room to call those men together, and if any are reported absent they will be brought to a Court Martial.

The Sergeants of the Companies are responsible that those men wear their coats turned the whole of the day.

This was a curious way of distinguishing a defaulter.

Lieut.-Colonel Disbrowe would appear to have been a hard punisher, and his powers seems to have been unlimited, from the following order.

27th February, 1807.

Lieut.-Colonel Disbrowe is very sorry to have such constant reports made of the misbehaviour of several of the men at Kew, and which obliges him to promise that in future every man so complained of shall be brought before a Court Martial. Thomas Poulton of Captain Wormeley's Company, would in this instance have been brought before a Court Martial ordered this day, but for some particular circumstances that appeared in his favour. Lieut.-Colonel Disbrowe therefore orders he may be confined in the black hole for twelve hours, and then confined to Barracks and drilled for six months. Samuel Barker of Captain Borrowe's Company, and Henry Whittaker of Captain Wolseley's Company, to be confined to Barracks and drilled for two months. Thomas Pearsell of Captain Swiney's, Charles Smith of Captain Neal's, John Stoke of Captain Burrowes's, Thomas Pritchard of Captain Whitby's, Samuel Ball of Captain Burrowes's, to be confined to Barracks and drilled for one month.

The price of shirts appears to have been somewhat exorbitant. The soldier of the present day could ill afford such a sum out of his slender pay.

25th April, 1809. R.O.

In consequence of the great rise in the price of linen, the men's shirts are to be charged to them at 7/- each, from the 25th inst.

20th May, 1809. R.O.

In order to encourage the men to take pains in firing at the target, the Commanding Officer of the Regiment directs that every man shall be passed over in his turn for guard in his company's roster for every time he hits the Target.

Indifferent as the shooting of the British soldier may be in the present day, it is at least infinitely superior to that of his predecessor in 1809 !

The following extract from orders appointing Mr. Askew J. Hillcoat to the Regiment will be interesting to those officers who knew him serving in 1881.

27th December, 1811. R.O.

Askew J. Hillcoat, gent., is appointed Lieutenant in the K. O. Stafford Militia, and is to do duty in Captain Colt's Company until further orders. Commission dated 25th December, 1811.

The following order records the death of the Earl of Uxbridge.

15th March, 1812. R.O.

Officers are requested to put on mourning for one month for the late Earl of Uxbridge.

The crape to be worn between the elbow and wrist on the left arm.

Lieut.-Colonel Newdigate is convinced that every officer and man will concur with him in lamenting the death of their respected Colonel, who during the 34 years he commanded the Regiment invariably promoted the interest and comfort of all ranks, and to whom are principally owing the reputation and distinguished honours which the Regiment has so long enjoyed.

The following order is a curious one.

29th April, 1813. R.O.

Although Lieut.-Colonel Newdigate has the most perfect confidence in the zeal and attention of the Detachment ordered to Norman Cross, he feels it his duty to mention the errors he is informed Regiments are apt to fall into on first taking that duty, viz :— That the prisoners always try (on the arrival of a fresh Regiment) whether they will be allowed to take liberties or not, by attempting to elude the vigilence of the sentries, and by bribing them to be careless on their duty.   Of that, however, Lieut.-Colonel Newdigate trusts there is but little danger.

But the offence most to be feared, and what has been often the cause of the reduction of non-commissioned officers, and the punishment of soldiers, is the very great temptation constantly offered by

the prisoners to procure straw for them to plaitt, and to smuggle
the plaitted straw out of prison, which is contrary to an express law,
and to the Standing Orders of the Garrison.

The following General Order from Horse Guards pro-
vides for a higher appointment of certain N.C.O'S. and first
institutes the rank of Colour-Sergeant.

General Orders,
Horse Guards,
6th July, 1813.

The Commander-in-Chief commands it to be declared in
General Orders, that His Royal Highness the Prince Regent, in
consideration of the Meritorious Services of the Non-commissioned
Officers of the Army, and with a view of extending encouragement
and advantages to those of the Infantry corresponding to the bene-
fit which the appointments of Troop Sergeant Majors offer in the
Cavalry, has been most graciously pleased in the name, and on
behalf of His Majesty, to direct that in all Regiments of Infantry
whose services are not subject to limitation, the pay of the
Serjeant Major shall henceforth be raised to three shillings per
day ; and that the pay of one Serjeant in each Company of the
Battalions of the above description, viz. :—Of those serving without limitation, shall be raised to two shillings and fourpence per
day, and that the said Serjeants shall be distinguished by an
Honourable Badge, of which, however, and the advantages attending
it, they will in case of misconduct be liable to be deprived at the
discretion of the Colonel, or Commanding Officer of the Regiment, or
by the sentence of a Court Martial.

In consequence of the above most gracious intimation of
His Royal Highness the Prince Regent's pleasure, the Commander-
in-Chief directs that the Serjeant selected for this distinction shall
be called the Colour-Serjeant, and that they shall bear above their
Chevron the Honourable Badge of a Regimental Colour supported
by Two Cross Swords.

It is His Royal Highness's pleasure that the duty of attending
the Colours in the Field shall at all times be performed by these
Serjeants, but that these distinctions shall in no wise interfere
with the regular performance of their Regimental and Company
duties.

The Commander-in-Chief recommends to the Colonels of
Regiments the utmost circumspection in the selection of the Colour-

Serjeants, and he hopes that this honourable appellation will invariably be bestowed on men of approved valour, distinguished by their attention to the duties of their station, and to the discipline of their respective companies.

The Commander-in-Chief avails himself of this opportunity of addressing himself to those who are the immediate objects of this order.

His Royal Highness entertains a just sense of the meritorious services of the Non-commissioned Officers of the Army, and he is persuaded that, under the directions of their officers, they have individually and collectively contributed largely to uphold the character of the British Army in its present pre-eminence ; and His Royal Highness rejoices most cordially that the services have been thus graciously noticed.

It may reasonably be expected that the reward which is thus held out to merit, will prove an incitement to all, for it is within the reach of all who have hands and hearts to serve their King and Country ; it is offered equally to the young as to the old soldier ; it is the recompense of honesty, sobriety, fidelity and personal bravery ; and His Royal Highness trusts it will prove the most powerful incentive to the Non-commissioned Officers of the British Army to persevere in that line of conduct which has obtained for them this munificent and distinguished favour from their country and sovereign.

By command of
His Royal Highness
The Commander-in-Chief.
(Signed) H. CALVERT,
Adjutant General.

From 1816 to 1852 the Militia Force was practically in 1816. abeyance, but from the latter date it sprung once more into existence in its present form, viz. : a Volunteer Militia.

The 1st King's Own Stafford Militia then assembled for 1852. 21 days' training at Stafford on the 9th November, under the command of Colonel the Earl of Dartmouth, and was dismissed on the 28th November the same year. The following officers were present, viz. : Colonel—The Earl of Dartmouth ; Lieut.-Colonel Giffard ; Major Inge ; Captains—Chambers, the Hon.

C. Wrottesley, Cavendish Taylor, and Challinor ; Lieutenants
—Hillcoat, Legge, Bunney, Willett, Simpson, Mousley and
Lane ; Ensigns—Astle, Neve, Mills, and Herford ; Captain
and Adjutant Hillman ; Surgeon Harland. Major the
Hon. W. P. M. Talbot was appointed to the Regiment from
the 7th Fusiliers before the end of the training.

1853. On the 1st April, Lieut.-Colonel the Hon. W. P. M.
Talbot was appointed to the command of the Regiment, and
on the 26th May following, the 1st King's Own Stafford
Militia assembled at Lichfield for 28 days' training. It was
inspected on the 21st June by Colonel Elliot, commanding
the 79th Highlanders, who expressed himself in most flattering
terms on the efficiency and manœuvring of the Regiment.
It was dismissed on the 22nd June. The following officers
trained with the Regiment :—Liet.-Colonel the Hon.
W. P. M. Talbot ; Majors Inge and Tennant : Captains—
Lord Lewisham, Hon. C. Wrottesley, Challinor, Fletcher,
S. Lane, Taylor, and Chambers ; Lieutenants—Hillcoat,
Stevens, C. Lane, J. P. Dyott, Willett, Mousley, Bunney,
and Eaton ; Ensigns—Neave, Astle and Elliot ; Captain and
Adjutant Hillman.

The same year the Regiment sustained a great loss in the
death of its Colonel, the Earl of Dartmouth ; and the following
letter was addressed to the Adjutant, Captain Hillman, on
the melancholy occasion by Lieut.-Colonel the Hon. W. P. M.
Talbot :—

KNOWSLEY, PRESCOTT,
28th November, 1853.

SIR,—It becomes my painful duty to announce to you, and through
you to the Regiment, the melancholy intelligence of the death of our
Colonel, the Earl of Dartmouth. The Regiment will, I am sure, be
desirous of testifying their respect and regret for this officer, who has

commanded them for a period of 40 years; and I have to acquaint you that, as a representative of the Corps, I have written to Captain Lord Lewisham to offer at the funeral the attendance of all the Officers, as well as of the Permanent Embodied Staff.

I have in reply received from Lord Lewisham a letter informing me that it was the wish of his father that he should be carried to the grave as unostentatiously as possible; and that the family would wish only the attendance of the six senior Officers of the Regiment as pall bearers. I have, therefore, to request that you will communicate with those Officers, and desire that they will report themselves to me at Patshull on Thursday, the 1st December, for the purpose of performing that melancholy duty. You will desire them to appear in full dress. The following Officers will be those on whom the duty will devolve :— Lieut.-Colonel Hon. W. P. Talbot, Major Charles Inge, Major George Tennant, Captain Francis Chambers, Captain Hon. Charles Wrottesley, and Captain Edward Challinor.

You will have the goodness to insert this letter in the Regimental Order Book, in order that a permanent record may be kept, testifying the deep regret which the Regiment feel at the loss of their old and much-respected Commanding Officer.

I am, Sir,
Your obedient Servant,
W. P. TALBOT, Lieut.-Colonel,
1st K.O. Stafford Militia.

The above-mentioned officers paraded at Patshull, and followed their late Colonel to the grave.

On the 20th April the Regiment assembled at Lichfield, 1854. the following officers being present :—Lieut.-Colonel Talbot ; Majors Inge and Tennant ; Captains—the Earl of Dartmouth, Hon. C. Wrottesley, Challinor, J. P. Dyott, Fletcher, Willett, Mousley, S. Lane, Taylor, and Chambers ; Lieutenants—Hillcoat, C. Lane, Neve, Taylor, Bunney, A'Court, Elliott, Eaton, Howard, and Pye ; Captain and Adjutant Hillman ; Surgeon Miller, and Assistant Surgeon Welchman. The Regiment numbered about 1,171 officers and men, and on the 4th May was presented with new colours by Lieut.-Col. the Hon. W. P. Talbot. These colours are at present carried by the 3rd Batt.

South Stafford Regiment. On the 5th May the Regiment furnished a Guard of Honour to receive the remains of Field-Marshall the Marquis of Anglesea, at 4-0 o'clock, p.m., at the "George" Hotel. On the 6th May, the Regiment lined the streets and formed a Guard of Honour during the funeral of the late Field Marshal, and on the 16th May, the following letter was received by Colonel Talbot :—

WHITEHALL,
15th May, 1854.

SIR —I am directed by Viscount Palmerston to inform you that an order will be sent this day to Her Majesty's Lieutenant for the County of Stafford, to extend the training of the 1st Staffordshire Regiment of Militia for one Week from Wednesday next, the 17th inst., which day the men would otherwise be dismissed.

I am, Sir,
Your obedient Servant.
HENRY FITZROY.

On the 16th May the Regiment was inspected by Colonel Reid, commanding the Midland district. and elicited from him the highest commendation.

After the inspection, Lieut.-Colonel the Hon. W. P. Talbot addressed the Regiment, and after reading to it the letter which he had received, by order of the Secretary of State, called upon the men to volunteer for the permanent service of Her Majesty, when all the officers and non-commissioned officers, and a large number of private soldiers, stepped to the front.

On the 24th May, the names of volunteers permitted to go on service were taken, and 645 men were selected for permanent service. On the 30th May the Regiment proceeded to Dover for the purpose of doing garrison duty in that town.

On the 13th October the Regiment was inspected at Dover by Colonel Pipon, the Assistant Adjutant-General, who expressed himself in terms of the highest praise of the discipline, steadiness, cleanliness and drill of the Regiment. On the 25th November, Colonel Talbot assembled the Regiment, and addressed it according to instructions he had received from Horse Guards, calling on the men to volunteer their services into the Line. Numbers of men came forward, and eventually 202 men were accepted. The total number of men given from the Regiment to the Line during this embodiment amounted to 1,200 (a whole Regiment), and for every 100 men given Colonel Talbot was permitted to nominate an officer to a commission in the Line. Thus many officers were transferred during this period to Line Battalions.

On the 17th January, Colonel Talbot again assembled 1855. the Regiment, and informed the men that the Queen had been pleased to select the Regiment as one of those to whom the offer was to be made to volunteer for service in the Mediterranean. Eventually 596 men volunteered, and the services of the Regiment were accepted. The 1st King's Own Stafford Militia was the first Regiment thus selected. Prior to its embarkation, the Regiment was inspected by Colonel Forster, on the 20th March, and, as a consequence of his report, the following letter was received from Horse Guards :—

HORSE GUARDS, 24th March, 1855.

SIR,—The General Commanding-in-Chief has received with much pleasure a highly favourable report of the Inspection of the 1st Stafford Militia made by Colonel Forster on the 20th inst., and I have the honour to request that you will communicate to the Regiment his Lordship's entire satisfaction at its discipline and efficiency, and at the general good conduct which has marked its residence at Dover. These results are most creditable to the manner in which you have administered the command of your Regiment, and the attention to their duties shown by both officers and men.

I have the honour to be, Sir,
Your obedient humble Servant,
G. A. WETHERELL, Adjutant-General.

On the 29th March, the Service Companies left Dover and embarked at Portsmouth on S.S. "Hansa," for conveyance to the Island of Corfu, where they arrived on the 13th April, 1855. On this voyage, about the 4th April, during Divine Service, an alarm of fire took place on board. The Regiment behaved with the utmost coolness and gallantry on this occasion, falling-in on deck in "open order," and without the slightest confusion, when ordered to do so by its officers, and remaining on parade till the fire was extinguished.

On the 15th April the Regiment landed, and was ordered to be stationed ot Fort Neuf Barracks. Shortly after its arrival at Corfu, the following letter was received by the Commanding Officer from Lord Hatherton, the Lord Lieutenant of the County, with reference to its embarkation at Portsmouth :—

PORTSMOUTH,

30th March, 1855.

SIR,—In transmitting the accompanying embarkation return of the 1st Stafford Militia Regiment on board the steamer " Hansa," I hold it my duty, and as justly due to that Corps, to bring under your notice for submission to the General Commanding-in-Chief, the highly soldier-like and creditable manner in which the embarkation of the Regiment was effected. The Officer in Command reported to me that not a man was either absent, drunk, or even late for parade on its quitting Dover early in the morning ; and the same state of good discipline existed on their arrival here, reflecting extreme credit on Colonel the Hon. W. P. Talbot and the other officers of the Regiment.

I have, etc.,

H. W. BRETON,

Major-General Commanding.

The Regiment was inspected on the 21st May the same year by Major-General McIntosh, who was afterwards pleased to issue the following Garrison order :—

The Major-General Commanding having this week inspected the Royal Stafford Militia on parade, has much pleasure in recording his satisfaction at the steadiness of the men under arms and correctness of manœuvre ; and he does not doubt that when he inspects their quarters, books, &c., he shall find their interior economy equal to their appearance on parade.

An order was received to send a detachment consisting of one captain, one subaltern, two sergeants, and forty-one rank and file, to Ithaca. This detachment was dispatched on the 5th August, under the command of Captain Rycroft.

On the 24th August, 1855, the Regiment embarked on board the screw steam Transport " Indiana," for Argostoli in the Island of Cephalonia, where it arrived on the 25th August, and disembarked under Lieut.-Colonel the Hon. W. P. Talbot the following day.

A detachment consisting of one captain, one subaltern, and fifty rank and file, was sent to Luxuri, under the command of Captain Cecil Lane, on the 26th August. Another detachment, consisting of one subaltern and thirty rank and file was sent, on the same day, to Fort George, under the command of Lieutenant Hillcoat.

During the Autumn of 1855, the Regiment suffered severely from the fever of the Country. Twenty-five men and three women and children died, and were buried at Trapano, where a stone was erected in their memory by their comrades.

The following address was presented on the 28th May, 1856. 1856, by the Regent of the Island, and the inhabitants of Argostoli and Luxuri, to the Regiment, being the first which had ever been conferred on any Regiment :—

32

ARGOSTOLI,
May 28th, 1856.

HONOURABLE SIR.—The people of Cephalonia, moved by a proper
sense of gratitude and respect towards you, expressed on a former
occasion how fortunate they considered themselves in having you
as a resident, but now that your departure and that of your Regiment
is fast approaching, they feel that the expression would be incomplete,
were they not to tell you how greatly they regret this occurrence.
As regards the Corps under your command this feeling is due to it
on account of the incomparable discipline and orderly spirit, which
it has displayed in this Island, as well as the singularly obliging
manner of the officers, who have so well imitated the example set to
them by their excellent Chief.

It may well be said, without fear of being accused of exaggera-
tion, that if under ordinary circumstances, familiarity and harmony
have existed between the Troops of Her Majesty and the people of
Cephalonia, it has never before been so great as it is at present, and
the feeling of regret which is felt by all classes at your departure
and that of your Regiment is quite unprecedented.

These feelings of sorrow are mitigated by the hope that you will
return among them, a hope which is founded on your well known
anxiety for the good of their Country and on the kindness of His
Excellency, the Lord High Commissioner, who certainly will not
deprive them of a Resident so generally loved and esteemed.

The absence of your Regiment will leave a blank which will
always be felt by the Cephalonians : and now that its departure is
imminent they have nothing but to accompany it with their best
and most sincere wishes for its glory and prosperity ; and so beg you
will accept these simple and heartfelt expressions, and that you will
kindly convey them to the distinguished Regiment under your command.

DEMETRIO, COUNT CARUSO,
Regent.

The following resolutions were received in June, 1856,
and read by Lieut.-Colonel the Hon. W. P. Talbot to the
men on a parade which was ordered for that purpose :—

HOUSE OF COMMONS,
Jovis 8 die Maii, 1856.

OPERATIONS OF THE LATE WAR.

Resolved—nemine contradicente.

That the thanks of this House be given to the officers of the
several Corps of Militia which have been embodied in Great Britain

and Ireland during the course of the War, for the zealous and meritorious service they have rendered to their Queen and Country at home and abroad.

Resolved—nemine contradicente.

That this House doth highly approve and ackowledge the services at home and abroad of the Non-Commissioned Officers and Men of the several Corps of Militia which have been embodied in Great Britain and Ireland during the course of the War, and that the same be communicated to them by the Colonels or Commanding Officers of the several Corps, who are desired to thank them for their meritorious conduct.

Ordered.

That Mr. Speaker do signify the said Resolutions respecting the Militia, by Letter, to Her Majesty's Lieutenant of each County, Riding, and Place, in Great Britain, and to His Excellency the Lord Lieutenant of that part of the United Kingdom called Ireland.

The Regiment remained at Argostoli during the Summer of 1856, and was again heavily visited by the fever which had attacked it severely the preceding year. At one period there were no less than 140 men in Hospital, among the 420 men who formed the Head Quarters of the Regiment at Argostoli.

On the 18th August, three companies under command of Major Inge received Orders to embark on board the steam transport " Mauritius," and to proceed to England. They arrived at Lichfield on the 16th September, after a long passage. The Head Quarters received its Orders on the 30th August, and embarked on board the steam transport " Prince Arthur," under command of Colonel the Hon. W. P. Talbot, and arrived at Lichfield on the 22nd September.

Captain Cecil Lane remained behind at Zante as British Resident, as a temporary measure.

The day following the arrival of the Head Quarters of the Regiment, Lieutenant-Colonel Talbot received the following address from the Magistrates of the City :—

We, the Magistrates of the City and County of Lichfield assembled at the Guildhall this day, cannot delay congratulating Colonel the Hon. W. P. Talbot and the officers and men of the several companies of the King's Own Stafford Militia upon their arrival at their Head Quarters in Lichfield, after eighteen months' service in the Ionian Islands.

It must be a source of pride and congratulation to this City, and the County at large, that this old and distinguished Regiment was *the first* to be *embodied* and *volunteer* for foreign service, and the *last* to be disembodied, at the same time adding to its colours " Mediterranean."

We likewise consider that the greatest praise is due to Lieut.-Col. W. P. Talbot and the Officers for the very efficient state and discipline of the Regiment.

The Magistrates also would not lose this opportunity of testifying their approbation of the soldier-like and orderly behaviour of the Depôt of the Regiment, which has for the period of eighteen months been billeted in this City, and most ably commanded by Major Tennant.

HALFORD W. HEWITT,
GUILDHALL,   Ex-Mayor and Chairman.
23rd Sept., 1856.

On the 27th September, 1856, Colonel Talbot received the Order for the disembodiment of the Regiment in a letter from Lord Hatherton :—

TEDDESLEY,
27th Sept., 1856.

SIR,—I have the honour of transmitting a Copy of a Warrant which Her Majesty has been pleased to issue, directing me to disembody the Regiment of Militia of this County under your command. I am commanded to signify to you Her Majesty's pleasure that it should be carried into execution on the 1st October next.

It is a very gratifying part of my duty to state that Her Majesty has, at the same time, commanded me to communicate to you and the Officers, Non-Commissioned Officers, Drummers, and Private Men, the high sense she entertains of their conduct, and of the zeal and spirit which they have manifested since they have been embodied.

I request that you will have the goodness to put the above paragraph into an Order of the Day.

I cannot conclude this communication without expressing to you my own thanks for the great attention you have paid to all my communications, and my conviction of the universal feeling of gratitude on the part of the County, for the trouble you have taken in forming and disciplining the Regiment under your command, and for the public spirit it manifested in volunteering for Foreign Service at a time when such services were of the greatest importance to the Country.

I should be glad if this expression on my part were also communicated to the Regiment.

I have the honour to be, Sir,
Your obedient Servant,
HATHERTON.

Before dismissing the men to their homes, Colonel Talbot published the following address to the Regiment :—

Lieut.-Colonel Talbot cannot publish the above order without congratulating the Regiment on the distinguished honour it has gained in having received this mark of Her Majesty's approbation.

Nor can he fail to express his satisfaction at the handsome terms in which the Lord Lieutenant expressed himself with regard to his own feelings, and that of the County at large, with reference to the services of the Regiment ; neither can he carry into effect the disembodiment of the Regiment without expressing to the Officers, Non-Commissioned Officers, and Men, his own most grateful thanks for the efficient manner in which all ranks have performed their several duties. Where all have equally exerted themselves to promote the efficiency of the Regiment, it would be invidious on the part of the Lieutenant-Colonel Commandant to specify the names of any particular officers among the junior ranks, but he feels it incumbent upon him to offer his thanks to Major Inge, who has invariably afforded him the most valuable assistance, as also to Major Tennant, who has maintained the Depôt Companies in a high state of discipline, notwithstanding the difficulties he has had to contend with in consequence of the men having been so long in billets.

To the different Officers of the Staff, Colonel Talbot cannot express in too high terms his sense of the untiring manner in which they have laboured to produce and maintain the discipline of the Regiment. Of Captain and Adjutant Hillman, Paymaster Mills, Ensign and Depôt Adjutant Oswell, Ensign and Quarter-Master O'Shea (whose death the Regiment has had to lament), he cannot

speak in too high terms ; nor can he withhold his special thanks
from the Medical Staff, who have had to perform most laborious
duties during the time the Regiment has been quartered in Cephalonia. For the period of eighteen months' service in the Ionian
Islands there have been no fewer than 712 cases of fever treated
and no less than 1717 cases have passed through the hospital, besides
women and children, while the deaths have amounted to only one
officer, twenty-nine men, five women and nine children. The Lieut.-
Colonel thinks that Surgeon Woodhouse, by his attention to the sick,
and the skill with which he has treated them, has earned the grateful remembrance of all who have been under his treatment, as well
as that of their relatives in this County.

The thanks of the Lieut.-Colonel Commandant, as well as of all the
Officers, are especially due to the Non-Commissioned Officers of the
Regiment, and particularly to the original Staff Sergeants, who, in
fact, have done the principal share of labour in the formation of the
Regiment, and paved the way for the discipline which has always
distinguished it.

To the Private Soldiers the Commanding Officer offers his heartfelt thanks for their uniformly steady, sober, and soldier-like, behaviour, and he cannot refrain from expressing his approbation of
their conduct, when, during two summers in the Island of Cephalonia,
they saw their comrades attacked with the malignant fever, and
dying around them, and yet cheerfully and without murmur performed the extra duties which devolved upon them, in consequence of
the great numbers of sick, varying from 90 to 140.

The Commanding Officer trusts that now the men are about to
return to their homes, they will not forget the lessons of orderly conduct, of sobriety, and of cleanliness, which they have received, and
that they will remember that they are still members of the 1st King's
Own Stafford Militia, and that as such, he and their Company
Officers will at all times take the liveliest interest in their welfare.

On the 1st October, 1856, the men were paid off, and
returned to their homes.

The undermentioned officers were present when the Regiment was disembodied, viz.:—

Lieut.-Colonel The Hon. W. P. Talbot ; Majors
Inge and Tennant ; Captains—Chambers, The Hon. C.
Wrottesley, Willett, Mousley, Rycroft, Eaton, J. P. Dyott,

and Bridgeman ; Lieutenants—Hillcoat, Taylor, Harrison, H. Talbot, Holyoake, Barnet, Jones, Marston, and Fitzgerald ; Ensigns —Severn, Owen, Boycott, Smith, and Neott ; Captain and Adjutant Hillman ; Surgeon Woodhouse ; Assistant-Surgeon Hitchins ; Quarter-Master Oswell.

The Regiment had then completed a service of two years and six months ; eleven months of which were passed in the garrison of Dover, and the remainder in the Ionian Islands.

On the 1st August, 1857, the Permanent Staff of the **1857.** Regiment was inspected by Colonel and Assistant Adjutant-General Douglas, who expressed himself highly gratified with the conduct, general regularity, and appearance of the Staff.

On the 15th October in the same year, Colonel Talbot received from the Lord Lieutenant of the County Her Majesty's Warrant that the Regiment should again be embodied for permanent service, and orders were given for the Regiment to assemble at Lichfield on the 3rd November, 1857. On that date the Regiment assembled at Lichfield, under command of Lieut.-Colonel The Hon. W. P. Talbot, and mustered 670 rank and file, notwithstanding that 200 men had received their discharge one month previously, having served their time.

On the 26th November, orders were received from Horse Guards to hold the Regiment in readiness to proceed to Perth and Stirling ; but subsequently fresh orders were sent to detach 300 men to Edinburgh Castle.

On the 30th November the Regiment paraded at 5 a.m., and halted at Carlisle for two hours, when the Regiment was mustered, and the detachment formed to proceed to Edinburgh Castle under Major Tennant.

The Head Quarters arrived at Perth on the morning of the 1st December. On the 9th and 10th December, the Head Quarters moved from Perth in two divisions, and proceeded to Edinburgh to be quartered there, Major Inge assuming the command. A detachment, consisting of two officers, four sergeants, and 100 rank and file were stationed at Greenlaw.

1858. The Regiment was inspected by Major-General Viscount Melville on the 5th February, and again on the 17th May, 1858. On the 10th August the Regiment received Orders to move from Edinburgh to Aldershot. It embarked on board the Troop Ship "Melbourne," and, arriving at Aldershot, it was encamped for six weeks on Cove Common, and subsequently moved into huts in L lines, North Camp.

The Regiment was inspected on the 7th October, 1858, by Major-General Lord William Paulett when he addressed the Regiment, and said it was equal to any he had commanded since he had assumed command of the 1st Brigade, and made several other remarks of a most complimentary description.

1859. The Regiment was specially selected to form a Guard of Honour to Her Majesty on the occasion of the opening of Wellington College, on the 29th January, 1859.

On the 12th May, 1859, the Regiment was again inspected by Major-General Lord William Paulett, on which occasion he highly complimented it for its internal arrangements, and also for its good conduct, drill, &c.

During its stay at Aldershot the 1st King's Own Stafford Militia formed part of the Division that was reviewed at that place by Her Most Gracious Majesty the Queen and the Prince Consort after the Indian Mutiny.

On the 18th September the Regiment moved to Portsmouth from Aldershot ; and, on its arrival, furnished five detachments, viz. : Gosport, Tipner, Anglesea, Clarence, and Cambridge Barracks : the Head Quarters being stationed at Colwort Barracks. Immediately after its arrival at Portsmouth, the following letters were received by Colonel Talbot—one from Lieut.-General Knollys, commanding the Division at Aldershot, and one from Major-General Lord William Paulett, commanding the 1st Brigade.

ALDERSHOT,
20th April, 1859.

MY DEAR COLONEL,—The 1st Stafford Militia having left my Command, I feel I am only performing an act of justice in requesting you to convey to the Officers, Non-Commissioned Officers and Privates the sense I entertain of their excellent conduct while forming part of the force. On inspecting them soon after their arrival, I took the opportunity of saying to them that I trusted, and doubted not, when the day of their departure arrived, I should only have to address them in terms of commendation. I was prevented doing this by urgent military duties, which called me to London on the day they marched to Portsmouth. I am therefore obliged to avail myself of this mode of assuring them that they have more than justified my expectations, and that their appearance and efficiency in the field have not been less gratifying than their orderly demeanour in quarters. I feel bound to add, in consequence, my obligations to yourself and Major Inge, and to all ranks of the 1st Stafford, particularly including Captain Hillman, the Adjutant, for the manner in which you and they have contributed to the credit of the Aldershot Division.
Believe me, my dear Colonel,
Yours very truly,
W. KNOLLYS.

NORTH CAMP, ALDERSHOT,
21st September, 1859.

MY DEAR COLONEL,—I regret very much that I was absent on a few days' leave when the 1st King's Own Stafford received their orders to move to Portsmouth, as I should have had great pleasure in expressing to you and the Regiment my regrets at parting with them, as they have always done my Brigade credit for the 14 months they have been under my command ; and I can assure you that, from the very efficient state I have always witnessed the Regiment, in their interior economy as well as on parade, the greatest credit is due to you, the Adjutant, Officers, Non-Commissioned Officers and men for keeping them in that state, more particularly as you have given so many men as Volunteers to the Line ; and I should feel obliged by your expressing these sentiments to the Regiment.

Believe me, very truly yours,
W. PAULETT, MAJOR-GENERAL,
Commanding 1st Brigade.

On the 27th October the Regiment was inspected by Major-General The Hon. Sir J. Yorke Scarlett, K.C.B., who expressed himself highly satisfied with the internal arrangements, as well as with the discipline and appearance of the Regiment.

The following appeared in the District Orders of the 5th November, 1859 :—

The Major-General has received the commands of His Royal Highness, the General Commanding-in-Chief, to notify in public Orders that of the parties lately under instruction at Hythe, that of the 1st Stafford Militia proved the best shooting detachment, and Private Jennings of that Regiment the best shot.

On the occasion of the launch of the new man-of-war, the "Victoria," on the 11th November, the 1st King's Own Stafford Militia furnished the Guard of Honour to Her Majesty, and lined the streets of Portsmouth.

On the 10th December, the following letter, written by desire of H.R.H. the Commander-in-Chief to Major-General The Hon. Sir J. Yorke Scarlett, K.C.B., Commanding the South-Western District, and transmitted by that officer, was received by Lieut.-Colonel The Hon. W. P. Talbot :—

HORSE GUARDS,
9th December, 1851.

SIR,—I have had the honour to submit to the General Commanding-in-Chief the Confidential and Autumn Inspection Reports of the embodied Regiments of Militia specified in the margin (1st King's Own Stafford Regiment), who are serving in the South-West District under your command, and I am instructed to convey to you the following remarks made thereon :—

Your report of this fine Regiment is exceedingly satisfactory to His Royal Highness.

The exemplary conduct of the men, evinced by the very few Courts Martial held in the Corps since the last Inspection, together with their efficiency and general appearance, prove this Regiment to be one of the best of the embodied force, and you will be so good as to express to Lieut.-Colonel The Hon. W. P. Talbot the high estimation in which His Royal Highness holds this Militia Corps.

BROOKE TAYLOR,
A.A. General.

The Regiment was inspected by Lord William Paulett 1860. on the 22nd May, 1860, when he once more expressed himself in the highest possible terms of the drill, the barracks, and the interior economy.

On the 29th May, a detachment, consisting of 1 field officer, 2 captains, 4 subalterns, and 152 rank and file, under command of Major Chambers, proceeded to Weymouth and Portland to relieve the East Kent Militia, who were recalled for the purpose of being disembodied. The detachment was further augmented by 2 officers and 127 rank and file on the 8th June, on the representation of insubordination amongst the convicts.

The Regiment was removed from Portsmouth and Weymouth on the 13th September, 1860, and sent to the Northern District. The Headquarters being at Newcastle-on-Tyne ; 4 companies, under Major Chambers, at Sunderland ; and 1 company, under Captain The Hon. C. Wrottesley, at Tynemouth. They remained there till the 27th November, when the Regiment was ordered to return to its County Head Quarters, when it was disembodied on the 30th November

1860.   On this occasion the 1st King's Own Stafford Militia had remained embodied for a period of three years.

1861.   During the year 1861 the Regiment was in a disembodied state, and the men were paid their bounties at the different towns where they resided, by the Adjutant, who went round for that purpose.

1862.   On the 8th day of May, 1862, the Regiment was mustered for training for 21 days, when 750 men were present, and received great praise from Major-General Wetherall for their attention and soldier-like bearing.

The Officers present were :—Lieut.-Colonel The Hon. W. P. Talbot ; Majors Inge and Chambers ; Captains— Hon. C. Wrottesley, C. Lane, Fletcher, Willett, Eaton, J.P. Dyott, Harrison, Lambarde, and Hervey Talbot ; Lieutenants —Hillcoat ; G.W. Moore, Dowie, Gledstanes, and Broomhead ; Captain and Adjutant Hillman ; Quarter-Master Oswell ; Surgeon Hitchens ; Assistant-Surgeon Hearnden.

1863   The Regiment assembled on the 24th April, 1863, for its training, and mustered 937 of all ranks.   At the termination of the training it was inspected by Colonel The Hon. G. Foley, who spoke in complimentary terms of the high state of the efficiency of the Regiment.

1864.   On the 21st April, 1864, the Regiment again assembled for training, and numbered 897 of all ranks, and was inspected by Colonel Adams of the 49th Regiment, who gave the Commanding Officer great credit for the high state of efficiency the Regiment had attained in so short a time.

Officers present :—Lieut.-Colonel the Hon. W. P. Talbot ; Majors Inge and Chambers ; Captains—The Hon. C. Wrottesley, Fletcher, Willett, Mousley, Eaton, J. P. Dyott,

Harrison, Hervey Talbot, and Dowie ; Lieutenants—Hillcoat,
Taylor, Broomhead, Gledstanes, and Elwes ; Captain and Adjutant Hillman ; Quarter-Master Oswell : Surgeon Hitchens,
and Assistant-Surgeon Welchman.

On the 1st May, 1865, the Regiment assembled for 27 **1865.**
days' training, when it mustered 801 of all ranks, and on the
25th of the month it was inspected by Lord Mark Kerr,
of the 13th Light Infantry, who expressed himself in the
most laudatory terms of the state of the Regiment.

The Officers present were Lieut.-Colonel the Hon. W.
P. Talbot ; Majors Chambers and the Hon. C. Wrottesley ;
Captains—Fletcher, Willett, Mousley, Dyott, Harrison, and
H. Talbot : Lieutenants—Hillcoat, Gledstanes, and Elwes ;
Captain and Adjutant Hillman ; Quarter-Master Oswell ;
Surgeon Hitchens, and Assistant Surgeon Hearnden.

The Regiment was called out for 27 days' training on **1866.**
16th April, 1866, when the muster was 719 of all ranks.   It
was inspected by Colonel Bingham, Assistant Adjutant-
General, Manchester, who expressed himself highly pleased
with everything he had seen, and said he should make a first-
class report to the Horse Guards.

The undermentioned officers were present, viz. :—Lieut.-
Colonel the Hon. W. P. Talbot ; Majors Chambers and
Hon. C. Wrottesley ; Captains—Fletcher, Willett, Mousley,
Eaton, C. Lane, J. P. Dyott, Harrison, H. Talbot, and
Dowie ; Lieutenants—Hillcoat, Elwes, Lloyd-Forster, and
W. G. Webb ; Captain and Adjutant Hillman ; Quarter-
Master Oswell ; Surgeon Hitchens, and Assistant-Surgeon
Welchman.

On the 6th May, 1867, the Regiment assembled for **1867.**
27 days' training and exercise, and mustered 721 of all ranks.

It was inspected on the 30th May, by Colonel J. W. Reynolds, Assistant Adjutant-General, Manchester, who said he
was very much satisfied with the high state of efficiency and
appearance of the Regiment, and that he would make a most
favourable report of the same.

The officers present during the training were Lieut.-
Colonel Hon. W. P. Talbot ; Majors Chambers and Fletcher ;
Captains—Willett, Mousley, C. Lane, Eaton, J. P. Dyott,
Harrison, H. Talbot, Dowie, and Elwes ; Lieutenants—Hill-
coat, Foster, and W. G. Webb ; Captain and Adjutant
Hillman ; Quarter-Master Oswell ; Surgeon Hitchens, and
Assistant-Surgeon Hearnden.

1868. The Regiment was called out for 27 days' drill and
training on the 27th April, 1868, at which period it mustered
17 officers and 841 rank and file. It was inspected on the
22nd May by Lieut.-Colonel H. Harpur Greer, C.B., of the
68th Durham Light Infantry, who expressed himself much
pleased with the Regiment, more especially as there were upwards of 250 recruits in the ranks.

The officers present were Lieut.-Colonel The Hon. W.
P. Talbot ; Majors Chambers and Fletcher ; Captains—
Willett, Mousley, C. Lane, J. P. Dyott, Harrison, H.
Talbot, Elwes, Foster, and W. G. Webb ; Lieutenants—
Hillcoat, Loneyan, and Elwell ; Captain and Adjutant Hill-
man ; Quarter-Master Oswell ; Surgeon Hitchens, and
Assistant-Surgeon Hearnden.

1869. The Recruits enrolled since the training of the Regiment
in 1868, attended at Lichfield on the 10th May, 1869, for
14 days' preliminary drill. The Regiment assembled on
the 24th May the same year for training, and mustered 17

officers and 981 rank and file. On the 17th June it was inspected by Lieut.-Colonel Deshon, when he expressed himself in very high terms of the manner the Regiment had gone through the different manœuvres, and the soldier-like appearance of the men generally.

The undermentioned officers were present, viz. :—Lieut.-Colonel The Hon. W. P. Talbot ; Majors Chambers and Fletcher ; Captains—Willett, Mousley, C. Lane, Harrison, H. Talbot, Elwes, Foster, and W. G. Webb ; Lieutenants—Hillcoat, Elwell, and Garnett ; Captain and Adjutant Hillman ; Quarter-Master Oswell ; Surgeon Hitchens, and Assistant-Surgeon Hearnden.

The recruits enrolled since the previous training attended 1870. at Lichfield for preliminary drill on the 18th April, 1870, and the Regiment assembled for 27 days' training on the 2nd May, when it mustered 21 officers and 1,005 non-commissioned officers and men. On the 23rd May the Regiment, commanded by Lieut.-Colonel Talbot, paraded in the Market Square, Lichfield, and proceeded by train to Stafford Common to take part in a field day with the 2nd and 3rd Stafford Regiments of Militia. It returned to Lichfield about 9-0 p.m. the same day. On the 25th May the Regiment was inspected by Colonel Campbell, of the 100th Regiment, who stated at the conclusion of the inspection that all he had seen had been done well, and that the most censorious could not find fault ; the appearance of the men was smart and soldier-like in the extreme ; the kits were in excellent order ; and the pouches well adjusted. The efficiency of the Regiment was a conclusive proof of the great attention which had been paid to the training, and he would have the greatest pleasure in presenting a favourable report to the War Office.

The following officers were present, viz. :—Colonel
The Hon. W. P. Talbot ; Majors Chambers and Fletcher ;
Captains—Willett, Mousley, C. Lane, Harrison, H. Talbot,
W. G. Webb, H. S. Stewart, and Arden ; Lieutenants—
Hillcoat, Elwell, Garnett, and M. H. Grazebrook ; Captain
and Adjutant Hillman ; Quarter-Master Oswell ; Surgeon
Hitchens, and Assistant-Surgeon Welchman.

1871.   On the 3rd April, 1871, the recruits enrolled since the
training of the Regiment in 1870 attended at Lichfield for
28 days' preliminary drill. The Regiment, under command of
Lieut.-Colonel The Hon. W. P. Talbot, assembled for 27
days' training on the 1st May, 1871, when it mustered 20
officers and 1,006 non-commissioned officers and men.
Colonel Campbell, of the 100th Regiment, again inspected on
the 24th May. He expressed himself in very high terms of
the manner the Regiment had gone through the different
manœuvres, and the soldier-like appearance of the men generally. He considered the Regiment had improved since the
last inspection, and he should report accordingly.

The following officers were present, viz :—Colonel The
Hon. W. P. Talbot ; Majors Chambers and Fletcher ;
Captains—Willett, Mousley, C. Lane, Harrison, H. Talbot,
E. H. Foster, W. G. Webb, Arden, and Garnett ; Lieuten-
ants—Hillcoat, Grazebrook, G. C. Talbot, and Townend ;
Captain and Adjutant Hillman ; Quarter-Master Oswell ;
Surgeon Hitchens, and Assistant-Surgeon Welchman.

1872.   The recruits enrolled since 1871 attended on the 25th
March, 1872, for 28 days' preliminary drill and instruction.
The Regiment, under command of Lieut.-Colonel The Hon.
W. P. Talbot, assembled for 27 days' training on the 22nd

April 1872, and mustered 24 officers and 1,020 non-commissioned officers and men. Colonel A. C. Robertson, of the 2nd Batt. 8th Foot, inspected the Regiment on the 17th May, and at the conclusion of the inspection said he had been much pleased with all he had seen ; the men had performed the various evolutions in the most satisfactory and steady manner. He particularly commended the attention in the ranks, and informed the men that their conduct in quarters had been good. This was the last year the 1st King's Own Stafford Militia assembled for training under Lieut.-Colonel the Hon. W. P. Talbot, who was on the 26th April of the following year appointed Honorary Colonel of the Regiment he had commanded for twenty years.

The following officers were present during the training :— Colonel The Hon. W. P. Talbot ; Majors Chambers and Fletcher ; Captains—Willett, Mousley, C. Lane, Harrison, W. G. Webb, Arden, and Garnett ; Lieutenants—Hillcoat, Grazebrooke, G. C. Talbot, Marshall, Hon. H. C. Legge, Oslear, Couran, Hon. W. F. Dawnay, Spring, and Hon. C. Finch ; Captain and Adjutant Hillman ; Quarter-Master Oswell ; Surgeon Hitchens, and Assistant-Surgeon Welchman.

On the 24th March, 1873, the recruits enrolled since the **1873.** previous training, assembled at Lichfield for 42 days' preliminary drill. The Regiment, under command of Major F. Chambers, assembled for 27 days' training on the 5th May, and mustered 23 officers and 1,058 non-commissioned officers and men. Colonel L. E. Knight, commanding the 19th Brigade Depôt, inspected the Regiment, and made the following report, viz. :—

The Officer commanding the 19th Brigade Depôt was much pleased with the steadiness on parade of the N.C.O. and men of the 1st Stafford Militia, which, in his opinion, reflects great credit on their commanding Officer, the Adjutant, and the Permanent Staff. He has also been greatly pleased with the quiet and orderly behaviour of the Regiment during its period of training, and the general absence of crime amongst it. The appearance of the Regiment is, in the opinion of the Officer commanding the 19th Brigade Depôt creditable to all concerned.

The following officers were present :—Majors Chambers and Fletcher ; Captains—Mousley, C. Lane, Harrison, Willett, H. Talbot, E. H. Foster, W. G. Webb, Arden, Garnett, and G. C. Talbot ; Lieutenants—Hillcoat, Grazebrook, Marshall, Oslear, Couran, Hon. W. F. Dawnay, and W. Wood ; Captain and Adjutant Hillman ; Surgeon Hitchens and Assistant Surgeon Welchman. Major Chambers was, on the 4th June appointed to the command of the Regiment.

1874. The recruits enrolled since the training of the Regiment in 1873, attended at Lichfield on the 23rd March, for 28 days' preliminary drill. The Regiment, under command of Lieut.-Colonel F. Chambers, assembled for 27 days' training on 27th of April, and mustered 21 officers and 1049 non-commissioned officers and men. Colonel L. E. Knight inspected the Regiment, and made the following report :—

Colonel Knight will have great pleasure in reporting to the Major-General commanding the Northern District the steadiness on parade and knowledge of their drill shown by all ranks of the 1st Stafford Militia, as well as their general good conduct in quarters and in camp, which is all the more creditable owing to its unexpected move into tents, which was done in a soldier-like manner. During its stay no complaints have been received from any of the neighbouring land-lords. Colonel Knight thinks this highly creditable to the colonel, adjutant, sergeants, and all concerned.

The following officers were present during the training :—Lieut.-Colonel Chambers ; Major Fletcher ; Captains—Willett,

Mousley, C. Lane, Harrison, H. Talbot, E. H. Foster,
W. G. Webb, Arden, Garnett, and G. C. Talbot ; Lieutenants
—Hillcoat, Grazebrook, Marshall, Oslear, Couran, Hon. W.
F. Dawnay, and W. Wood ; Captain and Adjutant Hillman ;
Surgeon Hitchens, and Assistant-Surgeon Welchman.

Owing to the large number of men in the 1st King's Own
Stafford Militia, it was decided by the Authorities that two
additional Companies should be raised, and the Regiment
divided into two Battalions. The order for carrying out this
arrangement was received an the 22nd August, 1874. Major
T. W. Fletcher, the junior Major, was appointed to the command of the 2nd Battalion, and the other transfers were as
follows, viz. :—Majors Mousley and Harrison ; Captains—
Webb, Arden, M. Grazebrook ; Lieutenants—the Hon. C.
Finch, and W. Wood.

The recruits enrolled since the training of the regiment 1875.
in 1874 attended at Lichfield on the 22nd March, 1875, for 28
days' preliminary drill. On the 19th April the 1st Battalion of
the Regiment, under command of Lieut.-Colonel Chambers,
assembled for 27 days' training, and mustered 16 officers and
651 non-commissioned officers and men. It was inspected
by Colonel F. Peyton, commanding 19th and 20th Brigade
Depôt, who called all the officers to the front, and expressed
his entire satisfaction with everything that had been brought
under his notice, and particularly praised the steadiness of all
on parade, and their good conduct during training. Colonel
Peyton also expressed his satisfaction at the great zeal and
tact of Captain and Adjutant D. Hillman, to whom the good
order and discipline of the 1st Battalion was much indebted.
He also spoke with great regret of Captain Hillman being about
to retire from the post which he had so long and so honour-

ably retained. Captain D. Hillman retired from the service
in November, 1875, after holding for 23 years the appointment of Adjutant to the 1st King's Own Stafford Militia, and
was succeeded by Captain and Brevet-Major F. B. N.
Craufurd, from the 80th Foot. The following officers were
present during the training of 1875 :—Colonel Chambers ;
Major C. Lane ; Captains—H. Talbot, E. H. Foster, Garnett,
Hon. W. F. Dawnay, Marshall ; Lieutenants—Hillcoat, and
Couran ; Sub-Lieutenants—Levett, Bissell, Whitby, C. E.
W.Wood ; Captain and Adjutant Hillman ; Surgeon Welch-
man, and Assistant-Surgeon Carter.

The 2nd Battalion of the Regiment assembled on the
31st May for 27 days' training, and was also inspected by
Colonel F. Peyton, who expressed his satisfaction at the
smart and soldier-like appearance of the Battalion. Square
was formed on the two centre companies, when the Inspecting
Officer gave the non-commissioned officers and men great
praise for their extremely good conduct during the training,
as well as for their steadiness under arms. The total numbers
present were 18 officers and 616 men. The 2nd Battalion
was disembodied on the 26th June.

The officers present were ;—Major Harrison ; Captains—
W. G. Webb, Arden, M. Grazebrook, Sneyd, K. O. Foster ;
Lieutenants—Hon. C. Finch, W. Wood ; Sub-Lieutenants—
N. T. Wood and Boyd. The Regimental Staff was the same
as for the 1st Battalion.

1876. On the 10th April, 1876, the recruits of both Battalions
enrolled since last training assembled at Lichfield for 55 days'
preliminary drill, and were dismissed on the 3rd June. There
were present 6 officers and 278 non-commissioned officers and
men.

On the 12th June, the two Battalions assembled at Lichfield, and were marched to Whittington Heath to be encamped for 27 days' training The 1st Battalion was inspected on 5th July, by Colonel Peyton, who said he was much pleased with the conduct of all under canvass, which, he remarked, was not only creditable to themselves, but a source of satisfaction to all those having authority over them. There were present of the 1st Battalion, 12 officers and 444 non-commissioned officers and men.

Colonel Chambers retired from the command of the Battalion in this year, and Colonel Harrison from the 2nd Battalion was appointed Colonel and Lieut.-Colonel Commandant. The following officers were present during the training, viz. :—Colonel Chambers ; Major H. Talbot ; Captains—Foster, Garnett, Marshall, and Captain W. G, Webb, attached from 2nd Battalion ; Lieutenants—Hillcoat, Bissell, Whitby, Birch, and Davies ; Brevet-Major and Adjutant Craufurd ; Surgeon Welchman.

The 2nd Battalion was inspected by Colonel Peyton at the same time and on the same day as the 1st Battalion, and the Inspecting Officer expressed himself extremely gratified with the state of the Battalion, which was most satisfactory in every way. The Battalion numbered 566 men and 14 officers.

The officers of the 2nd Battalion present during the training were :—Lieut.-Colonel Harrison ; Major D. Hillman ; Captains—W. G. Webb, M. Grazebrook, H. F. Sneyd, K. O. Foster, W. Wood ; Lieutenants—The Hon. C. Finch, W. Boyd, Hon. D. Finch, H. Lysons, Hon. W. Bagot, M. A. W. S. Broun, A. M. Thorneycroft. The officers of the Regimental Staff were the same as those for the 1st Battalion.

1877. On the 2nd April, 1877, the recruits of both Battalions, with a proportion of non-commissioned officers and men under Captain and Brevet-Major Craufurd, assembled for 55 days' preliminary drill ; they were paid off and returned to their homes on the 26th May. There were present 7 officers and 355 non-commissioned officers and men. The 1st Battalion under command of Colonel P. J. Harrison assembled at Lichfield on the 28th May, and numbered 14 officers and 463 non-commissioned officers and men. They were inspected by Colonel E. M. M. Buller, commanding 19th and 20th Brigade Depôt, on the 22nd June. Officers present :—Colonel Harrison ; Major W. G. Webb ; Captains—Hon. C. W. Finch, and Bissell ; Lieutenants—Hillcoat, Hon. D. Finch, Davies, Henderson, and St. Leger-Wood ; Brevet-Major and Adjutant Craufurd.

The 2nd Battalion, under command of Lieut.-Colonel H. Talbot, assembled at Lichfield on the 1st July, and consisted of 14 officers and 453 men. The Battalion was inspected by Colonel E. M. M. Buller on the 27th July, and the following Battalion Order was published by Colonel H. Talbot :—

The Commanding Officer has much pleasure in publishing in Orders the high satisfaction expressed by Colonel E. M. M. Buller, 19th and 20th Brigade Depôts, at the manner in which the Battalion acquitted itself at the inspection, and in which he fully concurs.

The Battalion was dismissed on the 28th July. The undermentioned officers were present during the training, viz. : Lieut.-Colonel H. Talbot ; Major E. H. Foster ; Captains—Arden, M. Grazebrook, K. O. Foster ; Lieutenants —Whitby, L. T. Birch, Lysons, Hon. W. Bagot, M. A. W. S. Broun, Thorneycroft, Campbell, St. Leger Wood. Lieutenant H. M. Nuthall, 58th Regiment, acted as Adjutant to the 2nd Battalion during this training.

The recruits of both Battalions who had enrolled since 1878. 1877, assembled on the 25th March, 1878, for 55 days' preliminary drill and training. They are described as being " a fine body of men, both in size and physique, and their conduct during their training was such as to gain for them the goodwill of the inhabitants of the City of Lichfield."

On the 3rd April, 1878, owing to a period of imminent National danger, Her Majesty's Proclamation was issued, calling up the Reserves for mobilization. In compliance with this Proclamation, the Militia Reserve belonging to the 1st Battalion 1st Stafford Militia was summoned to attend at Lichfield on or before the 20th April, 1878, for Army Service. In consequence of the numbers reporting themselves before that date (the billeting accommodation being limited as the recruits were up for preliminary drill), a detachment, consisting of 25 non-commissioned officers and men, was sent to Dublin to be attached for Army Service to the 38th (1st Staffordshire) Regiment, and on the 29th April another party, consisting of 72 non-commissioned officers and men, was sent to join the same Regiment.

On the 26th April, 1878, H.R.H. the Field Marshal Commanding-in-Chief, in pursuance of the Queen's command, issued a General Order, expressing Her Majesty's high opinion of the very satisfactory manner in which the men of the Army Militia Reserve had responded to the call made on them to join the Army for permanent service.

The period of National emergency having passed, the Militia Reserves, by an order dated July 20th, 1878, were ordered to return to their homes, and in compliance with this order, the men numbering 104 returned to Lichfield from

Army Service, were paid off, and sent by rail to their various destinations.

The 1st Battalion under command of Colonel Harrison, assembled at Lichfield on the 27th May, 1878, for 27 days' training, and was marched to Whittington Heath to be encamped there. Owing to the absence of the Militia Reserve on Army Service, and the large number of recruits who had been dismissed to their homes, the assembly was a very weak one. It was inspected by Colonel E. M. M. Buller on the 21st June, who addressed the Battalion in very favourable terms, and said he would make a most favourable report of what he had seen. Total present :—10 officers, and 346 non-commissioned officers and men. The officers present during the training were :—Colonel Harrison ; Major W. G. Webb ; Captains—Marshall, Hon. C. W. Finch, and Bissell ; Lieutenants—Hon. D. Finch, Davies, Henderson, Finlay, and St. Leger-Wood ; Brevet-Major and Adjutant Craufurd.

The 2nd Battalion assembled at Lichfield on the same date as the 1st Battalion, and was also encamped on Whittington Heath. It was under the command of Colonel H. Talbot, and numbered 16 officers and 503 men. The Battalion was inspected by Colonel E. M. M. Buller at the same time as the 1st Battalion, and the Inspecting Officer's remarks were of an equally complimentary nature.

The officers present were :—Lieut.-Colonel H. Talbot ; Major E. H. Foster ; Captains—Arden, M. Grazebrook, L. T. Birch, H. T. Sneyd, K. O. Foster, W. Wood ; Lieutenants—A. Hillcoat, M. A. W. S. Broun, Campbell, Hon. W. Bagot, and Sub-Lieutenant Tennant ; 2nd Lieutenants— Sir H. H. E. Chamberlain and A. C. Talbot. Captain Wortham, of the 64th Regiment, officiated as Adjutant.

55

The recruits of both Battalions who had enrolled since <inline type="margin">1879.</inline>
the training of 1878, assembled at Lichfield on the 14th
April, 1879, for preliminary drill and training. The 1st
Battalion, under command of Colonel Harrison, assembled at
Lichfield on the 26th May, and was marched to Whittington
Heath to be encamped there for 20 days' training. It
was inspected on the 11th June by Colonel Buller, who
expressed his satisfaction with everything he saw. There
were 14 officers and 592 non-commissioned officers and men.
The officers present were :—Colonel Harrison ; Major W.
G. Webb ; Captains—Hon. C. W. Finch, Bissell, Whitby,
and M. A. W. S. Broun ; Lieutenants—Hon. D. Finch, and
Finlay ; Second Lieutenants—Cooch, Jackson, Hon. C.
Finch, Blacklock, T. E. Hickman ; Brevet-Major and Adjutant Craufurd.

The 2nd Battalion, under command of Colonel H.
Talbot, assembled at Lichfield on the same date as the
1st Battalion, and was encamped with it on Whittington
Heath. The 2nd Battalion was inspected by Colonel Buller
at the same time as the 1st Battalion. There were present
14 officers and 608 men.

The officers were :—Lieut.-Colonel H. Talbot ; Major
E. H. Foster ; Captains—Grazebrook, L. T. Birch, H.
Sneyd, K. O. Foster, W. Wood ; Lieutenants—A. Hillcoat,
Hon. W. Bagot, E. Tennant ; 2nd Lieutenants—Sir H. H.
E. Chamberlain, A. C. Talbot, and S. Harrison. Lieutenant
Oakley, of the 1st Battalion 8th Regiment, acted as Adjutant
during this training.

On the 16th February, 1880, a letter was received from <inline type="margin">1880.</inline>
Horse Guards directing that both the 1st and 2nd Bat-
talions of the 1st King's Own Stafford Regiment should be

augmented by two companies. On the retirement of Colonel Harrison this year, Colonel Hervey Talbot, from the 2nd Battalion, succeeded to the command of the 1st Battalion, and was appointed Lieut.-Colonel Commandant of both Battalions.

The recruits who had enrolled since the previous training, assembled at Lichfield on the 12th April, 1880, for preliminary drill and training under Captain and Brevet-Major Craufurd.

The 1st Battalion, under command of Colonel Hervey Talbot, assembled at Lichfield on the 24th May, 1880, for 27 days' preliminary training, and was marched out to Whittington Heath to be encamped there. It was inspected by Colonel E. M. Buller on the 15th June. At the close of the inspection, the Inspecting Officer stated that he was highly satisfied with the drilling, the appearance, and the conduct of the Battalion. Total present, 15 officers, and 748 non-commissioned officers and men. The following officers were present during the training :— Colonel Hervey Talbot ; Major Arden, from the 2nd Battalion ; Captains—Marshall, M. A. W. S. Broun, Nuthall, and Finlay ; Lieutenants—Cooch, Jackson, and Blacklock ; 2nd Lieutenants—Hon. A. Bethell, Law, Lawrence, Galt, and McSwiney ; Brevet-Major and Adjutant Craufurd.

The 2nd Battalion, under command of Major W. G. Webb, assembled for training on the same date as the 1st Battalion, and the two Battalions were encamped together on Whittington Heath. The 2nd Battalion was inspected by Colonel E. M. M. Buller on the 15th June, and he expressed himself much pleased. Total present, 18 officers and 763 non-commissioned officers and men.

The officers present were :—Major W. G. Webb; Captains—Grazebrook, Birch, Sneyd, K. O. Foster, W. Wood; Lieutenants—A. Hillcoat, Hon. C. Finch, Tennant, Talbot, S. Harrison, T. E. Hickman; 2nd Lieutenants—Denison, F. Charrington, Sturges, Plevins, Maclurcan. Lieutenant A. Paget of the 68th Light Infantry, officiated as Adjutant to the Battalion.

On the 25th September Lieut.-Colonel Eustace, late Lieut.-Colonel 60th Foot, was appointed to the command of the 2nd Battalion.

The recruits of both Battalions assembled at Lichfield 1881. on the 23rd May, 1881, and the 1st Battalion King's Own Stafford Militia, under Colonel Hervey Talbot, assembled on the 20th June, and was quartered in Whittington Barracks for 27 days' training. The Battalion mustered 18 officers and 741 non-commissioned officers and men, and was inspected by Colonel E. M. M. Buller previous to being dismissed.

The officers present were :—Colonel H. Talbot; Major W. G. Webb; Captains—Hon. C. Finch, M. A.W. S. Broun, Nuthall, A. Finlay, and J. B. Price; Lieutenants—Hon. D. Finch, H. S. Wood, Jackson, Blacklock, Law, and Galt; 2nd Lieutenants—Goren, E. V. D. Pearse, C. S. Talbot, and W. Arden; Captain and Adjutant Kell.

The 2nd Battalion, under command of Lieut.-Colonel Eustace, also assembled for training on the 20th June, and was encamped on Whittington Heath. It was inspected by Colonel Buller on the 14th July, and dismissed on the following day.

The officers present were :—Colonel Eustace ; Major M. Grazebrook ; Captains—K. O. Foster, Wood, Spooner,

Winter, Chamier, Denison, Tennant ; Lieutenants—Charrington, Plevins, Galt, McSwiney ; 2nd Lieutenants—Oliver, Wyley, Burton, and Denison. Lieutenant St. George, of the 38th Regiment, acted as Adjutant to the 2nd Battalion during the training.

The following General Order, dated the 11th April, 1881, was promulgated for the organization of the Infantry of the Line and the Militia.

ORGANIZATION.—The Infantry of the Line and the Militia will in future be orgauized in Territorial Regiments, each of four battalions for England, Scotland, and Wales, and five Battalions for Ireland, the 1st and 2nd of these being Line battalions, and the remainder Militia. These Regiments will wear a territorial designation, corresponding to the localities with which they are connected.

By a subsequent order the 38th and 80th Regiments became the 1st and 2nd Battalions of the South Staffordshire Regiment, and the 1st and 2nd Battalions of the 1st King's Own Stafford Militia were linked to these Line Battalions as the 3rd and 4th Battalions respectively of the same Regiment, and the facings of the Regiment were changed to white.

The Regiment sustained a great and irreparable loss in January this year by the death of Lieutenant Askew Hillcoat. This officer received his first commission in 1811, when the King's Own Stafford Militia was quartered at Windsor under King George III., and was in receipt of a pension from the Government. At the time of his death he had 70 years' service as a subaltern in the Regiment, for had he accepted promotion he would have forfeited his pension. His loss was greatly deplored by every officer in the Regiment, for his death severed the last link which connected the present South Stafford Militia with the old 1st King's Own Stafford Militia of King George III.'s time.

The 3rd Battalion South Staffordshire Regiment, late 1st 1882. Battalion 1st King's Own Stafford Militia, assembled at Lichfield on the 8th May, 1882, under command of Colonel Hervey Talbot, for 27 days' training, and was encamped on Whittington Heath. It was inspected on the 1st June by Colonel H. R. L. Newdigate, C.B., commanding the Regimental District. There were present, 17 officers, and 692 non-commissioned officers and men. The following are the names of the officers :—Colonel H. Talbot ; Majors—W. G. Webb, and Hon. C. Finch ; Captains—M. A. W. S. Broun, A. Finlay, J. B. Price, Hon. D. Finch and Jackson ; Lieutenants—Blacklock, Pearse, Law, Talbot, Christie, Bowlby, and Bird ; Quarter-Master T. Trout. Captain and Adjutant Kell.

The 4th Battalion South Staffordshire Regiment, under command of Colonel Eustace, assembled at Lichfield on the 8th May for the annual training, and was quartered in Whittington Barracks, and was inspected on the same day as the 3rd Battalion by Colonel Newdigate, C.B.

The following officers were present :—Colonel Eustace ; Majors—M. Grazebrook, K. O. Foster ; Captains—Spooner, Winter, Chamier, Deinson, Tennant ; Lieutenants—Hon. C. Finch, Sturges, Charrington, Plevins, Oliver, Maclurcan, Denison, Wyley, McSwiney. Captain W. T. Cautley, of the 1st Battalion, officiated as Adjutant.

The 3rd Battalion assembled at Whittington Heath 1883. Barracks on the 11th June, 1883, for 27 days' training, under Colonel Hervey Talbot, and was inspected by Colonel H. R. L. Newdigate, C.B. They mustered 17 officers and 609 non-commissioned officers and men. The following are the officers who were present during the training of the Battalion,

viz. :—Colonel H. Talbot ; Major W. G. Webb ; Captains—
M. A. W. S. Broun, Nuthall, A. Finlay, J. B. Price, Black-
lock, and Biggs-Baldwin ; Lieutenants—E. V. D. Pearse,
Burton-Phillipson, Brooke, H. B. Christie, Bowlby, N. O. B.
Chamberlain, and E. de R. Jervis ; Captain and Adjutant
Kell ; Quarter-Master T. Trout.

On the 29th May the establishment of the 3rd and 4th
Battalions was augmented by one Adjutant, and Major W.
S. Darley, 1st Battalion, was appointed Adjutant of the
4th.

The 4th Battalion assembled in Whittington Camp,
under command of Colonel Eustace, on the 11th June, and
on the 5th July was inspected by Colonel Newdigate, C.B.
Total present, 14 officers and 710 non-commissioned officers
and men.

The undermentioned officers were present during the
training :—Colonel Eustace ; Majors—Grazebrook, K. O.
Foster ; Captains—Winter, S. Denison, F. Charrington,
Jameson, Newell ; Lieutenants—McSwiney, Plevins, Wyley,
Burton, and E. Denison ; and Major and Adjutant W. S.
Darley.

1884.   In 1884, the 3rd Battalion assembled once more under
the command of Colonel Hervey Talbot on the 16th June,
and was encamped on Whittington Heath. It was
inspected on the 10th July by Colonel W. D. Scrase Dickins,
commanding 38/64 Regimental Districts. There were 13
officers and 574 non-commissioned officers and men present.
The following are the names of the officers :—Colonel H.
Talbot ; Majors—W. G. Webb, and Hon. C. Finch ;
Captains—M. A. W. S. Broun, A. Finlay, J. B. Price, and

Blacklock ; Lieutenants—Pearse, Brook, N. Chamberlain, and E. de R. Jervis ; Major and Adjutant Kell ; Quarter-Master T. Trout.

The Regiment sustained a severe loss in the death of its commanding officer, Colonel Hervey Talbot, which took place on the 11th September, 1884, at his private residence, Aston Grange, Preston Brook, Cheshire. His coffin was carried to the grave by a party of non-commissioned officers from the 3rd and 4th Battalions, who were anxious to pay this last mark of respect to their late Colonel.

Colonel Hervey Talbot was succeeded in the command of the 3rd Battalion by Colonel R. J. E. Eustace, from the 4th Battalion, who thus became Lieut.-Colonel Commandant of both Battalions.

On the 16th June the 4th Battalion assembled under command of Colonel Eustace in Whittington Barracks for 27 days' training, and was inspected by Colonel Dickins on the 9th July. Present, 10 officers and 605 non-commissioned officers and men.

Officers present :—Colonel Eustace ; Captains—Winter and Charrington, who officiated as Majors ; Captains—Jameson, Newell, E. E. Denison, and McSwiney ; Lieutenants—Miller, Elkington ; Major and Adjutant W. S. Darley.

The 3rd Battalion, under command of Colonel R. J. E. **1885.** Eustace, assembled at Whittington Barracks on the 6th July, 1885, for 27 days' training. On its assembly the following Regimental order was published to both Battalions :—

The Colonel Commandant cannot again meet the Regiment without placing on record his deep sense of the great loss it has sustained since the last training, by the death of Colonel Hervey Talbot, a regret which is shared by every officer and soldier of the 3rd and 4th Battalions, who knew and appreciated his many social and soldierly qualities.

Colonel Talbot had served for 25 years in the Reguler Army and Militia. No officer was more proud of his command, or took a deeper interest in the welfare with everything connected with the South Staffordshire Militia and its long history.

Colonel Eustace trusts that he will receive the same cordial support from the officers, non-commissioned officers, and men, which they always accorded to Colonel Talbot, and that the Regiment will continue to maintain under his command the high character it has deservedly enjoyed for so many years.

The Battalion was inspected on the 29th July by Colonel Scrase Dickins, and mustered 20 officers and 702 non-commissioned officers and men.

The following were the officers present :—Colonel Eustace ; Majors—The Earl of Aylesford and M.A.S. Broun ; Captains —J. B. Price, Hon. D. Finch, Blacklock, Biggs-Baldwin, E. E. A. Denison, and E. V. D. Pearse ; Lieutenants—N. Chamberlain, Jervis, C. Eustace, C. Fitz-Clarence, E. Fitz-Clarence, Boynton, Tarte, W. F. Christie, and W. D. Hickman ; Major and Adjutant Kell ; and Quarter-Master T. Trout.

The 4th Battalion, under command of Lieut.-Colonel W. G. Webb, assembled for its annual training on the 6th July, and was inspected on the 30th of that month by Colonel Dickins, commanding the 38/64 Regimental District. Numbers present, 13 officers and 615 non-commissioned officers and men.

The following officers were present, viz. :—Lieut.-Colonel W. G. Webb ; Majors—Grazebrook and Finlay ; Captains—S. Denison, F. Charrington, Newell, McSwiney, Captain and Hon Major Hargreave ; Lieutenants—Miller, A. Chetwynd, Jellicorse, and J. H. Moore ; Major and Adjutant W. S. Darley.

The 3rd Battalion South Staffordshire Regiment, under **1886.** command of Colonel Eustace, assembled at Lichfield for 27 days' training on the 31st May, 1886, and was encamped on Whittington Heath. It was inspected by Colonel Scrase Dickins, and mustered 19 officers and 721 non-commissioned officers and men.

The following were the officers present :—Colonel Eustace ; Majors Swinfen-Broun and Price ; Captains—The Hon. D. Finch, Blacklock, Biggs-Baldwin, Pearse, Chamberlain, and Hon.-Major Kell ; Lieutenants—Jervis, Eustace, Boynton, Christie, Weld-Forester, Ricardo, Howard Wrigley, and Talbot ; Captain and Adjutant Sandham ; and Lieut. and Quarter-Master Trout.

The 4th Battalion, under command of Colonel W. G. Webb, assembled at Whittington Barracks for 27 days' training on the 31st May, and was inspected on the 24th June by Colonel Dickins. Total present, 14 officers and 616 non-commissioned officers and men.

The officers of the Battalion present during the training were :—Colonel W. G. Webb ; Majors—Grazebrook, and A. Finlay ; Captains—Hon. Major Winter, Charrington, Newell, McSwiney, Hon. Major Hargreave ; Lieutenants—Miller, Jellicorse, A. Chetwynd, Lindesay, and Abbott ; Major and Adjutant W. S. Darley.

On the 6th June the 4th Battalion, under command of **1887.** Colonel W. G. Webb, assembled at Whittington Barracks. On the 21st June the Battalion took part in the celebration of Her Majesty's Jubilee on Whittington Heath. On the 1st July it was inspected by Colonel Dickins, and was dismissed on the 2nd July. There were present 20 officers and 616 non-commissioned officers and men.

64

The following officers were present :—Colonel W. G.
Webb ; Majors—Grazebrook and A. Finlay ; Captains—
Denison, Charrington, Hon. Major Winter, Hon. Major
Hargreave, Tennant, A. Chetwynd, B. Seckham, Newell ;
Lieutenants—Lindesay, Abbott, F. D. Hickman, J. H.
Moore, Buller, Bond, Challenor, and Lane ; Major and
Adjutant W. S. Darley.

On the 4th July, 1887, the 3rd Battalion, under Colonel
Eustace, assembled at Whittington Barracks. It was
inspected by Colonel Scrase Dickins, and the men were dismissed to their homes on the 30th July. There were present
23 officers and 677 non-commissioned officers and men.

The officers present were :—Colonel Eustace ; Majors—
Swinfen-Broun and Price ; Captains—Blacklock, Biggs-Bald-
win, Pearse, Chamberlain, Hon.-Major Kell, Jervis, and
Hamilton ; Lieutenants—Eustace, W. F. Christie, Weld-
Forester, Ricardo, H. Wrigley, Talbot, Fellows, Allen,
Ionides, Browne, and H. R. Christie ; Captain and Adjutant
Sandham and Lieut. and Quarter-Master Trout.

1888. The 3rd Battalion, under command of Colonel Eustace,
assembled at Lichfield on the 7th May, 1888, for 27 days'
training, and was encamped on Whittington Heath. It
was inspected by Colonel C. G. Heathcote, Commanding
38/64 Regimental District, on the 31st May. The Battalion
mustered 20 officers, and 637 non-commissioned officers and
men. The undermentioned officers were present :—Colonel
Eustace ; Majors—Swinfen-Broun and Price ; Captains—
Blacklock, Biggs-Baldwin, Pearse, Chamberlain, Hon.-Major
Kell, Jervis, and Hamilton ; Lieutenants—Eustace, W. F.
Christie, Weld-Forester, H. Wrigley, Talbot, Fellows, Allen,
Ionides, Browne, H. R. Christie, and S. J. Jervis ; Captain

and Adjutant Sandham ; Lieut. and Quarter-Master Trout.

The 4th Battalion, under Colonel W. G. Webb, assembled at Whittington Barracks on the 4th June, and on the 28th of the same month was inspected by Colonel C. G. Heathcote, commanding 38/64 Regimental District, and was dismissed on the 30th June.   Numbers present, 21 officers and 633 non-commissioned officers and men.

The officers present were :—Colonel W. G. Webb ; Major A. Finlay ; Captain and Hon. Major Winter, who officiated as Major during the training ; Captains—Denison, Charrington, Captain and Hon. Major Newell, Hon. Major Hargreave, Tennant, B. Seckham ; Lieutenants—Challenor, Hickman, Lane, Bond, Hall, J. H. Moore, Mark, Butler, Owen, Wilkinson, Stewart ;   and Captain and Adjutant C. Way.

By the death of Colonel Eustace, Commandant 3rd and 4th Battalions South Staffordshire Regiment, on the 1st April, 1889, Colonel W. G. Webb succeeded him as Lieut.-Colonel Commandant of both Battalions, but retained the command of his own, the 4th Battalion.

On the 29th April, 1889, the 3rd Battalion, under command of Major Swinfen-Broun assembled at Whittington Heath Barracks. It was inspected by Colonel Heathcote and the men were dismissed to their homes on the 25th May. The Battalion mustered 20 officers and 655 non-commissioned officers and men.

The following were the officers present :—Majors—

Swinfen-Broun and Price ; Captains—Blacklock, Hon. Major
Biggs-Baldwin, Pearse, Chamberlain, Hon. Major Kell, Jervis,
Hamilton, and Broadwood ; Lieutenants—W. F. Christie,
Weld-Forester, H. Wrigley, Fellows, Allen, Browne, H. R.
Christie, S. J. Jervis, Leader, and Moseley ; Captain and
Adjutant Sandham ; Captain and Quarter-Master Trout.

On the 24th June the 4th Battalion, under Colonel W.
G. Webb, assembled at Whittington Barracks for its annual
training, and was inspected on the 16th July by Colonel
C. G. Heathcote.   Total present, 21 officers and 603 non-
commissioned officers and men.

The officers present were :—Colonel W. G. Webb ;
Majors—Grazebrook and A. Finlay ; Captains—Hon. Major
Winter, Charrington, Hon. Major Newell, Hon. Major Har-
greave, Tennant, Seckham, J. H. Moore ; Lieutenants—
Butler, Lane, Owen, Hall, Wilkinson, Stewart ; 2nd
Lieutenants—Eustace, Dove, Williams, Wimberley. Captain
Curling, of the 1st Battalion Durham Light Infantry,
officiated as Adjutant during the training.

1890.   On the 26th May the 4th Battalion, under the command
of Colonel W. G. Webb, assembled at Whittington Barracks
for 27 days' training, and on the 19th June was inspected
by Colonel C. G. Heathcote, and was dismissed on the 21st
June.   Numbers present, 22 officers and 578 non-commissioned officers and men.

The following officers were present:—Colonel W.G.Webb;
Majors—A. Finlay and Winter ; Captains—Charrington,
Hon. Major Newell, Hon. Major Hargreave,Tennant, Seckham,
F. D. Hickman, J. H. Moore, H. Wrigley ; Lieutenants—

Lane, Hall, Wilkinson, Dove, Owen, Williams, Eustace : 2nd
Lieutenants—Wimberley, Saunders-Davies, Horsefield : and
Captain and Adjutant F. Geddard.

The 3rd Battalion assembled at Whittington Barracks on
21st July, 1899, for its annual training, when the command
was assumed by Colonel M. H. Graniewick, from the 4th
Battalion, in succession to Colonel Eustace, deceased.   The
numbers present were 20 officers, and 577 men, together with
28 permanent staff, and 59 recruits at drill at the Depôt.
The Battalion was inspected by Colonel Heathcote.   The
officers present were :—Colonel M. Graniewick : Majors—
Swinfen-Brown, and Hon. Lieut.-Colonel Prim : Captains—
(Hon. Major) Biggs-Baldwin, Pearse, Chamberlain, Hamilton,
Broadwood, and the Hon. R. Cheteryni : Lieutenants—W.
F. Christie, H. R. Christie, Leader, and Mooney : 2nd
Lieutenants—Wilson, Grahame, Garrard, Smith, and Evans :
Captain and Adjutant Saudham : Captain and Quarter-
Master Trout.

The recruits of the 4th Battalion received their last non-
training assembled at Lichfield for their course of musketry
instruction on 13th April.

The 4th Battalion, under command of Colonel W. G.
Webb, assembled at Whittington Barracks on the 27th April,
for its annual training.   It was inspected by Colonel C. G.
Heathcote on the 21st May, and dismissed on the 23rd May.
Total present during the training, 20 officers and 639 non-
commissioned officers and men.

The undermentioned officers were present, Lieut.-Colonel
W. G. Webb ; Majors—A. Finlay and Courtenay : Cap-

tains— Hon. Major Newell, Hon. Major Hargreave, Tennant,
Hickman, J. H. Moore, Eustace ; Lieutenants—Lane,
Williams, Mark, Dove, Hall, Wilkinson, Hounsfield,
Saunders-Davies ; 2nd Lieutenants—Foster and Knowles ;
Captain and Adjutant F. Geldard.

The recruits of the 3rd Battalion raised since May, 1890,
assembled at Whittington Barracks on the 8th June, 1891,
for 14 days' instruction in Musketry, prior to the training.

The 3rd Battalion, under command of Colonel M. H.
Grazebrook, assembled at the same place, on the 21st June.
The numbers were 16 officers, 26 permanent staff, and 535
men, and in addition there were 78 recruits at the Depôt. The
Battalion was inspected by Colonel Heathcote. Owing to the
paucity of officers, there were attached from other Militia
Battalions, 1 major, 3 captains, and 3 subalterns. The officers
of the Battalion present at the training were :—Colonel M.
Grazebrook ; Major Swinfen-Broun ; Captains—Pearse,
Chamberlain, Hamilton, and the Hon. R. Chetwynd ; Lieu-
tenants—Leader, Moseley, Grahame, Garrard, Smith, Evans ;
2nd Lieutenant Bousfield ; Captain and Adjutant C. H.
Wylly ; Captain and Quarter-Master Trout.

In this year Her Majesty Queen Victoria was most
graciously pleased to present to Colonel Webb and the
Officers of the 3rd and 4th Battalions South Staffordshire
Regiment, through Sir Henry Ponsonby, a photogravure of
the picture of herself and the Prince Consort reviewing the
Aldershot Division after the Indian Mutiny in 1859, the 1st
King's Own Stafford Militia having been amongst the troops
reviewed on that occasion. This picture is much valued by

the Officers of the Regiment, and has the following inscription :—

THE QUEEN AND PRINCE CONSORT
AT THE CAMP AT ALDERSHOT, 1859.

PRESENTED IN 1891
TO THE 3RD & 4TH BATTALION SOUTH STAFFORDSHIRE REGIMENT,
BY
HER MAJESTY QUEEN VICTORIA,

as being one of the Regiments which took part in the Review, by Her Majesty, of the Aldershot Division in 1859 after the Indian Mutiny, under its then name of the 1st King's Own Stafford Militia, commanded by Colonel the Honble. W. P. Talbot.

The recruits of the 3rd Battalion raised since the previous 1892. training, to the number of 191, assembled at Lichfield on the 16th May, 1892, and proceeded by rail to camp at Altcar, near Liverpool, the same evening, for their 14 days' course of Musketry.

The 3rd Battalion, under command of Major Swinfen-Broun, assembled on the 30th May, and also proceeded the same evening to camp at Altcar, for 27 days' training. The Battalion mustered 15 officers, 29 permanent staff, and 631 men. It was inspected by Colonel C. G. Heathcote, on the 24th June, and returned to Lichfield the following day, and were dismissed to their homes. The following officers were present :—Major Swinfen-Broun ; Captains—(Hon. Major) Biggs-Baldwin, Pearse, Chamberlain, Hamilton, The Hon. R. Chetwynd, Challenor, and H. C. Wrigley ; Lieutenants— Grahame, Garrard, Smith, and Bousfield ; 2nd Lieutenant Mason ; Captain and Adjutant C. H. Wylly ; Captain and Quarter-Master Trout.

The recruits enrolled since the previous training assembled at Lichfield on the 11th July, and went through their musketry course of instruction at Stafford.

The 4th Battalion, under General W. G. Webb, assembled at Whittington Barracks on the 25th July, and were inspected by Colonel C. G. Heathcote on the 18th August. There were present 20 officers and 670 non-commissioned officers and men.

The following officers were present during the training, viz. :—Colonel W. G. Webb ; Majors A. Finlay, F. Charrington ; Captains—Hon. Major Newell, Hon. Major Hargreave, Seckham, Tennant, Hickman, Hall ; Lieutenants—Lane, Williams, Dove, Saunders-Davies, Knowles, Foster ; 2nd Lieutenants—Loder-Symonds, Macnamara, and Fowler ; Captain and Adjutant Geldard.

Colonel M. H. Grazebrook, Commanding 3rd Battalion South Staffordshire Regiment, died at his residence at Southsea, on the 12th November, and was followed to the grave by Major Swinfen-Broun, Captain and Adjutant Wylly, and eight of the Permanent Staff of the Battalion, who acted as pall bearers. On the 10th December, Major Swinfen-Broun was gazetted Lieut.-Colonel and succeeded to the command of the 3rd Battalion.

1893. The Battalion assembled at Whittington Barracks on 24th June, and was inspected by Colonel Raper, 20th July. The following officers were present :—Colonel Webb ; Majors Finlay and Charrington ; Captains and Hon. Major—Newell, B. Seckham, Tennant, Hickman, Hall, Lane, and Williams ; Lieutenants— Knowles, Foster, Symonds, Macnamara,

Mossop, D. Seckham, Moss, Knox, Routledge, and Townson;
Captain and Adjutant Geldard.

The Battalion assembled for their training at Whitting- 1894.
ton Barracks on June 4th, and was inspected June 28th by
Colonel A. G. Raper, commanding Regimental District.
The following officers were present :—Colonel Webb ; Major
Charrington ; Captains—B. Seckham, Tennant, Hall, Lane,
Williams, Saunders-Davies, and Evans ; Lieutenants—
Foster, Macnamara, D. Seckham, Moss, Knox, Routledge,
Townson, Talbot, Smith, and Rycroft ; Captain and Adjutant
Geldard.

.The 4th Battalion assembled on May 6th for their 1895.
annual training, and went into camp on Whittington Heath.
On May 24th Colonel Raper had a brigade parade drill, and
a *feu-de-joie* was fired in honour of the Queen's Birthday.
This was the first occasion on which the 4th Battalion had
been on parade with its 1st Battalion, the latter being then
quartered in the Barracks. Inspection of the Battalion took
place on the 28th, when Colonel Raper expressed himself
much pleased with all he saw. The following officers were
present :—Colonel Webb ; Majors Finlay and Charrington ;
Captains—B. Seckham, Tennant, Hall, Lane, Saunders-
Davies, Hickman, and Mossop ; Lieutenants—Foster,
Macnamara, D. Seckham, Moss, Knox, Routledge, Townson,
Rycroft, Smith, and Danks ; Captain and Adjutant Going.

The Regiment assembled under Colonel W. G. Webb, at 1896.
Lichfield, on August 10th, and the same day left for Aldershot, where it was encamped on Danger Hill. It formed
part of the Division commanded by Major-General Lord
Methuen, C.B. Manœuvres took place lasting about a week,

and on September 11th the Regiment took part in a grand review, at which over 25,000 troops were present. During the Regiment's stay at Aldershot it earned much praise for its soldier-like behaviour, and its general smartness on parade and in camp. It returned to Lichfield on September 12th, and the men were dismissed to their homes.

The following officers were present :—Colonel Webb ; Majors Finlay and Charrington ; Captains—B. Seckham, Tennant, Hall, Saunders-Davies, Hickman, and Williams ; Lieutenants—Knox, Rycroft, Smith, Danks, Sadlier-Jackson, and Scobell ; Captain and Adjutant Going.

1897.　The Regiment assembled on May 10th, at Lichfield, and proceeded to Leominster the same day, where it went into camp. Owing to the excellence of the rifle range much time was devoted to musketry, with satisfactory results. The inspection took place on May 28th and 29th, by Colonel J. E. H. Prior, who had lately succeeded to the command of 38/64th Regimental District. The following officers were present :—Colonel Webb ; Major Charrington ; Captains and Hon. Majors Seckham and Tennant ; Captains— Hickman, Williams, Saunders-Davies, and Hughes ; Lieutenants—Rycroft, Danks, Smith, Sadlier-Jackson, Scobell, and Grigg ; Captain and Adjutant Going.

1896.　The Regiment assembled on August 8th, at Lichfield, and proceeded to Leominster the same day, where it went into camp. On August 22nd, Major-General Swaine, commanding the North-Western District, inspected the Regiment, and was pleased to express his great satisfaction with all that he saw. On August 26th the Regiment proceeded to Salisbury, where it went into camp at Homington, during the assembly of the troops who comprised the

Northern Army, and who were to take part in the manœuvres. The Regiment was in the Brigade commanded by Major-General Fitzroy Hart, C.B., and amongst the other Regiments in the Brigade was the 1st South Staffordshire Regiment. On August 26th the 4th Battalion took part in a Brigade Drill under General Hart, who was much pleased with the smartness of the Regiment on parade. The manœuvres began on September 1st, and lasted till the 9th. The heat during the whole time was excessive, and very trying to all concerned, as long marches had to be made, and fresh camps pitched every day. A grand review of the forces engaged took place on the 9th, and the Regiment returned to Lichfield on the 10th, and the men were then dismissed to their homes. The following officers were present :—Colonel Webb. C.B. ; Lieutenant-Colonel Finlay ; Major Charrington ; Captains and Hon. Majors Seckham and Tennant ; Captains Williams and Hughes ; Lieutenants—Rycroft, Smith, Hodgson, Grigg, Colchester-Wemyss, and Rendall ; Captain and Adjutant Going ; Quartermaster Penketh.

In September, 1898, Colonel the Hon. W. P. Talbot, who was appointed Honorary Colonel of the 1st King's Own Stafford Militia in 1873, died and was buried at Esher, his funeral being attended by many of the Officers and Non-Commissioned Officers past and present of both the 3rd and 4th Battalions.

Colonel W. G. Webb, C.B., who had been Colonel-Commandant of the 3rd and 4th Battalions since 1889, retired, and was succeeded in the command of the 4th Battalion by Major F. Charrington. Colonel M. A. Swinfen-Broun became Colonel Commandant of the two Battalions until 1900, when they became two separate Regiments.

1896. The Regiment was called up for its annual training on July 2nd, and assembled at Lichfield, and the same day entrained for Leominster, where it remained in camp until the 26th. The inspection took place on the 26th, when Colonel J. E. H. Prior, commanding 38/64 Regimental District, expressed himself highly satisfied with the efficiency of the Regiment.

The War in South Africa, which commenced in October, 1899, having assumed larger proportions than was originally expected, Her Majesty's Government gave orders for certain Militia Regiments to be embodied to relieve Line Battalions which were to be sent to South Africa. The 4th South Staffordshire Regiment were included in the first list selected for that duty, and were ordered to be embodied on December 5th. They were the only Regiment selected that had not one of their Line Battalions engaged in the War, and this was looked upon as a great compliment to the Regiment.

The Regiment assembled at Lichfield on December 5th, to the number of 706 officers and men, and left the same night for Kinsale. A large crowd assembled in the streets of Lichfield, and gave the men a hearty "send-off."

They embarked at Milford Haven, and arrived at Cork on the morning of the 7th. Two companies were at once sent to Spike Island, and one company to Fort Camden, Queenstown Harbour; the remainder went on to Kinsale, where Head Quarters and 4 companies took over the barracks, and one company occupied Fort Charles, commanding the entrance to Kinsale Harbour. The news of three reverses in South Africa caused great feelings of anxiety in England, and on December 23rd Lieutenant-Colonel Charrington having paraded the Regiment, asked the men if they were willing to volunteer for active service in South Africa; the whole Regiment, with great enthusiasm, volunteered to a man, and shortly afterwards the Secretary of State for War wrote and thanked the Regiment for their patriotic offer.

On January 29th orders came for the Regiment to hold 1900. itself in readiness to embark for South Africa on February 10th. Great enthusiasm ensued. Subsequently the date of sailing was altered to February 12th, and on the morning of that day Head Quarters and detachment from Fort Charles left Kinsale at 8 a.m. for Cork, and proceeded to Queenstown, where it was met by the three outlying companies, and embarked on the transport "Arundel Castle." The crew of the Flagship H.M.S. "Howe" manned the yards, their band played patriotic airs, and amidst great cheering from the ships in the harbour and the crowds on shore, the transport sailed about 3 p.m., with orders to proceed with all possible speed to Cape Town. The following officers sailed :— Lieutenant-Colonel Charrington ; Majors B. T. Seckham and E. W. Tennant; Captains—G. Williams, H. Saunders-Davies, R. Le G. Elers, P. E. F. Smith, and J. H. Ridgway ; Lieutenants—G. H. Whitehouse, H. D. Balfour, L. P. Reeves, P. W. Brookes, J. M. Stewart, and E. G. Howell ; Second Lieutenants—H. Clover, J. H. Rymer, G. C. Deans, P. L. Russell, A. L. Martin, and L. D. Inglefield ; Captain and Adjutant E. A. Bulwer ; Lieutenant and Quartermaster J. Penketh ; and Captain R. A. Lewis, R.A.M.C. Also the following attached officers :—Captain G. Seckham, 3rd North Staffords ; Captain J. B. Aiken, 5th Manchester Regiment ; Captain H. B. Hughes being left behind on sick leave, was subsequently transferred to the

3rd South Staffordshire Regiment. The number of non-commissioned officers and men who embarked was :— Warrant Officers, Staff Sergeants, and Permanent Staff, 7 ; Sergeants, 19 ; Corporals, 29 ; Drummers, 16 ; Privates, 530—Total 615.

The Battalion disembarked at Cape Town on 8th March and proceeded to Kimberley the same day, arriving there on 11th March. 23 officers, and 602 non-commissioned officers and men ; Lieutenant Reeves and 8 non-commissioned officers and men of the machine-gun section followed by a later ship. On 16th March, Head Quarters with "A. B. E. and G. Companies" went to Modder River relieving Head Quarters, and half Battalion of 2nd Northampton Regiment there. "C. D. F. and H. Companies," under Major Seckham left Kimberley on 24th March, with a Column under Lord Methuen, reaching Barkley West on 26th, and Likatlong on 28th, and leaving the latter place on the following day, reached Dronfield on 31st, and remained there till joined on 3rd April by Head Quarters and the half Battalion from Modder River, who were relieved by 3rd Battalion King's Own Scottish Borderers. Whilst at Dronfield, " B. and F. Companies" were quartered at Riverton Pumping Station on the Vaal, and "C. and D. Companies" at Macfarlane's Farm on the railway.

In April, the Battalion was brigaded in 20th Brigade under General Paget. On 3rd May, Head Quarters and half Battalion proceeded to Warrenton to take part in the forcing of the Vaal at Fourteen Streams. There was an Artillery action on 4th May, and a demonstration of all troops eastwards from Warrenton, whilst General Hunter moved on

Fourteen Streams, north of the Vaal. Owing to a mistake in orders sent to General Paget, the Battalion had to return suddenly to Kimberley at 9-30 that night, returning to Dronfield on 7th May. The Battalion concentrated at Dronfield on 9th May, and moved to Kimberley, and left there with 4th Scottish Rifles for Boshof on 10th May, where they arrived on 12th. The 1st Division (9th and 20th Brigades), under Lord Methuen, were concentrated there, and left on the 14th and 15th, reaching Hoopstad on 19th, Bothaville on 25th, and Kroonstad on 29th. Lord Methuen with 9th Brigade, left Kroonstad on 30th for Lindley, to the relief of 13th Imperial Yeomanry; and 20th Brigade followed next day, reaching Lindley on 3rd June, and was then left to garrison that place.

In the dispositions for the defence of Lindley the Battalion covered the south-east and south. The enemy "sniped" continually every day and started shelling on 16th. On 21st June, an attack was made on Munster Picquets and there was heavy firing all day, and the convoy which arrived from Kroonstad had had hard fighting all the way in. Supplies at this time in Lindley were getting very low. On 22nd June there was heavy "sniping" and shelling all day. The morning of the 26th of June opened with very brisk "sniping"; about 1 p.m. heavy firing commenced, and shelling from 3 guns, on our Picquets, the Scottish Rifles and Yorkshire Light Infantry No. 1 Picquet, and several hundred Boers appeared from the east and came galloping up, and a heavy attack then began to develop on the north-east corner, held by a Picquet of Yorkshire Light Infantry which was very hard pressed and had 13 out of the 15 men in the trench, killed or wounded; Private Ward, King's Own Yorkshire

Light Infantry, here won a V. C. for carrying a message for
reinforcements, which arrived and saved the situation. No.
7 Picquet held by "E" Company, 4th South Staffords, came
under and maintained a heavy fire, supported from the trenches
at the Head Quarters bivouac. Private Wilkinson was
severely wounded, having his arm broken, and whilst lying on
the ground was again shot at by a Boer a few yards off,
inflicting a severe wound in the thigh; the enemy were even‐
tually driven off and retired towards evening, the casualties to
the garrison being, 6 killed and 22 wounded. On 27th a
large convoy with reinforcements arrived from Kroonstad,
having had hard fighting all the way. On the 2nd July, all
the mounted troops left Lindley, moving east, and clearing
the country towards Leeuw Kop, this Battalion demonstrated
on the ridge, east of the town, and the machine gun came into
action, accounting for 2 or 3 Boers.

On the 3rd July, Lindley was evacuated, the Infantry
moving towards Leeuw Kop, where the Boers had a position
which General Paget attacked and carried, the 38th Battery
losing heavily; the enemy retired on Bethlehem. On the 4th,
5th, and 6th July the column moved towards Bethlehem, which
was strongly held by the enemy, and together with Major-
General Clement's Brigade commenced the attack on it on
6th and continued it on the 7th, when the enemy evacuated
the place, losing a gun, captured by the Royal Irish. During
the attack on Bethlehem two Companies of this Battalion
were escort to two five-inch guns, two Companies covered the
left flank of the attack, and the remainder of the Battalion
guarded the convoy and rear. Entered Bethlehem on the 8th,
and remained there till the 15th, when 20th Brigade moved out
about 6 miles on the Senekal Road, being joined by General

Broadwood's Cavalry Brigade, on 16th, the idea being to inter-
cept De Wet, who had broken out of Brandwater Valley at
Slabbert's Nek. Only came up with his rearguard which held
strong positions, and he got away with his force. During the
fight the Battalion with some Tasmanian Bushmen covered
the convoy, and came under shell fire from a gun which the
Boers moved round to the left rear.

On the 17th July, a column composed of half Battalion
King's Own Yorkshire Light Infantry, 4th South Staffordshire Regiment, and two Companies of Scottish Rifles, 2
guns, C.I.V., and some Tasmanian Bushmen, left Bullfontein
under Colonel Barter, with a large empty convoy for Winburg,
where it arrived on the 21st. The same force with full convoy
left Winburg on 24th July, and arrived without opposition at
Slabbert's Nek on 30th, where the news was heard of
Prinsloo's surrender with 4,000 Boers.

On 4th August, 20th Brigade left Slabbert's Nek in
charge of 2,500 prisoners, the 4th South Stafford Regiment
being put in charge of the Wepener Commando of about 550
Boers, marched daily viâ Senekal, and arrived at Winburg on
the 9th, and that evening 100 men of the Battalion left by
train for Cape Town with 500 prisoners. The whole
Battalion went down to Cape Town by daily detachments in
charge of prisoners and not a single man escaped.

At Winburg a draft of 115 men from home of 4th
Battalion arrived, and 150 men of the 1st Battalion to be
attached for duty, the latter remaining with this Battalion
till its departure from South Africa.

The whole Battalion returned to Winburg for garrison duty, and Colonel Charrington was for some time Commandant there; strength of the garrison about 1,500 men.

The 3rd and 4th Battalions were separated by the following order published in the "London Gazette, 17th July, 1900" :—

Her Majesty has been graciously pleased to approve, with effect from 1st August, 1900, of the division into two separated and distinct units of the under-mentioned double Battalions of Militia, viz :— " 3rd and 4th South Staffordshire Regiments."

On August 23rd, Colonel Ridley left Winburg with the Queenstown Volunteers on a reconnaissance towards Ventersburg ; they were surrounded by the enemy at Helpmakaar Farm, and sustained heavy losses, but held out till morning of 26th, when relieved by General Bruce-Hamilton's Column. At daylight on 27th August, firing suddenly commenced from Yeoman Kopje, a detached Kopje north of Winburg, which was then held by a draft of the Manchester Regiment and 50 men of this Battalion.   A large force of Boers was seen advancing with 2 or 3 guns from farm north-west, apparently unconscious that Yeoman Kopje was occupied ; our men withheld their fire as long as possible, but as the Boers suddenly scattered out they opened on them, emptying several saddles and hitting several horses.   The enemy then retired their guns behind the farm and opened fire on Yeoman Kopje, but did no damage.

A small patrol of Queenstown Volunteers cleverly captured Olivier, who was in command of the Boers, and his sons and brought them in to Winburg.   The enemy also made an attack on east and south-east of the town, but reinforcements from Bruce-Hamilton's Brigade appearing they retired at all points. During September, the Boers were continually round Winburg in varying strength, and on 18th October they blew up all the culverts on the Winburg-Smaldeel line, and did great damage to the permanent way.

On 19th October, Colonel Charrington commanding the 4th South Staffordshire Regiment, accompanied by the Rev. Harman, Wesleyan Minister, drove out and had an interview with Haasbroek, the Boer Commandant, regarding two men of his Commando who were being tried for murder in Bloemfontein. On the morning of 20th October, the enemy fired some well-directed shells into the Head Quarter camp of the Battalion from a ridge north-east, but did no damage. On 22nd, the railway was again destroyed and there was no train service for many weeks.

Towards the end of January, De Wet passed east and 1901. west of Winburg moving south to Cape Colony, being pursued by General C. Knox. On 28th February a column was formed from Winburg, under Major Pine-Coffin, consisting of 100 Driscoll Scouts, 40 Malta Mounted Infantry, 2 guns, 9th Battery Royal Field Artillery, and 3 officers (Captain Aiken, Lieutenants Deans and Martin), and 160 men 4th South Staffordshire Regiment, and moved out towards Doornberg, to co-operate with Colonel Williams. The column occupied Ventersberg and did good work, the detachment of this Battalion returning on 18th March, reporting casualties of 3 men "missing" in the Doornberg, and Private Banks who died at Ventersberg Road Station.

On 6th April, the Boers in force attacked No 2 Railway Picquet, at 3 a.m., 6 miles from Smaldeel, and held by 1 non-commissioned officer and 15 men of the Battalion ; but after two hours' heavy firing the Boers were driven off with several casualties.   Private Bourne, " B " Company was severely wounded : the enemy destroyed the line and then went on to No. 3 Picquet and captured the non-commissioned officer and 10 men holding it, having crept up in a mealie field.   These men, with those " missing " in the Doornberg were eventually released at Volksrust on 3rd May.   On 11th June, Sergeant Allen and 9 men of " C " Company were captured by the enemy whilst on Cattle Guard, and were released near Leribe on 22nd June.

The 3rd South Stafford Regiment embarked at Southampton on 17th June, on board the " Bavarian " for South Africa.

On 6th July, the news came that 5th Battalion Manchester Regiment, which had also come out in the " Bavarian," was coming up to relieve the Battalion at Winburg, and it arrived on 15th.

The Battalion left by special train at 6-45 a.m., on 16th, marching out strength : 15 officers and 512 non-commissioned officers and men, and arrived at Cape Town about 11 a.m. on 19th, embarking immediately on the transport " Lake Erie," which sailed at 4 p.m.   No other troops were on board except a few details, Colonel Charrington commanding 4th Battalion was in command of the troops, and Captain Owen-Jones in charge of the ship.   Nothing eventful occurred during the voyage home, and the " Lake Erie " arrived at Southampton early on Saturday morning, 10th August, where orders were received that the Battalion had to remain on board till Sunday night, and at 10 p.m. that night it left for Lichfield by special train, arriving about 7 a.m. on Monday, 12th August.

There were many friends of the Regiment waiting at the station to welcome it, and the station yards and approaches were crowded. The Battalion was formed up as soon as possible in line in the street, and headed by the Band of 4th Provisional Battalion marched along St. John Street, Bore Street, the Market Place, and Dam Street, through the Close to the Museum Grounds, where long rows of tables had been erected, and a bountiful supply of refreshments provided by the generosity and kindly thought of the inhabitants of Lichfield and its neighbourhood. The Mayor (Mr. Haynes) in a short and suitable speech welcomed the Regiment home ; and Colonel Charrington replied, and thanked the Mayor and Citizens of Lichfield for their warm welcome and kindness to the Regiment which would never be forgotten. At the call of the Mayor, cheers were given for the Colonel and the Regiment, and the Regiment in turn gave hearty cheers for the Mayor and Citizens of Lichfield. The Regiment then marched through the City, which was gaily decorated and crowded with friends and relatives, and reached Whittington Barracks, and as soon as possible everything was handed in, and the Battalion was disembodied after a little more than 20 months' service.

The following is the roll of the non-commissioned officers and men of the Battalion who died in South Africa.

No.	Rank.	Name.	Date of Death.	Cause of Death.
4129	L-Sgt.	R. Daniels	31st March, 1900	Accidentally drowned (In Vaal River)
4473	Pte.	J. Benton	20th April ,,	Enteric
4355	,,	J. Palmer	21st May ,,	,,
4550	,,	F. Dixon	20th ,, ,,	,,

No.	Rank.	Name.	Date of Death.			Cause of Death.
1458	Pte.	C. Chapman	22nd May,	1900		Enteric.
4544	L-Sgt.	J. Hemsley	23rd ,,	,,		,,
4523	Pte.	G. Armstrong	29th ,,	,,		,,
1984	,,	D. Mullins	13th ,,	,,		,,
4892	Cpl.	C. Hodgkins	1st June	,,		,,
2541	Sgt.Dr.	T. Simpson	17th ,,	,,		,,
4681	Pte.	W. Lawley	7th ,,	,,		,,
4918	,,	W. Bagnall	2nd ,,	,,		,,
5161	,,	J. Clarke	8th ,,	,,		,,
4974	,,	F. Willis	6th ,,	,,		,,
3125	,,	J. Newell	17th ,,	,,		,,
4784	,,	M. Collett	8th July	,,		,,
4521	,,	T. Howell	8th Aug.	,,		,,
5354	,,	E. Pike	16th Dec.	,,		,,
4385	,,	T. Hollamby	18th ,,	,,		,,
3845	,,	T. Morris	3rd Feb.	1901		,,
4639	Sgt.	H. Walker	8th ,,	,,		,,
5243	Pte.	C. Wells	8th ,,	,,		,,
5321	,,	E. Yates	25th ,,	,,		,,
4838	,,	R. Haynes	27th ,,	,,		,,
5082	,,	A. Moulton	22nd ,,	,,		,,
5309	,,	A. Hobbins	2nd March	,,		,,
4449	,,	S. Hogan	5th ,,	,,		,,
4824	,,	W. Tranter	13th ,,	,,		,,
2978	Drmr.	E. Ballinger	16th ,,	,,		,,
4830	Pte.	F. Ford	16th ,,	,,		,,
5043	,,	Isaac Banks	17th ,,	,,		,,
4057	,,	G. Hughes	23rd ,,	,,		,,
4015	,,	J. Sylvester	21st April	,,		,,
2288	,,	A. Gidlow	27th ,,	,,		,,
5182	,,	A. Haynes	30th ,,	,,		,,
4964	,,	W. Phillbrook	20th May	,,		,,
4065	,,	J. Evans .	31st ,,	,,		,,
4637	,,	S. Lounds	9th June	,,		,,
2719	L-Cpl.	A. Smith				,,
5137	Pte.	P. Mannion	4th July,	1900		Accidentally shot
4863	,,	E. Picken	23rd April,	1901		Died of Wounds

In Lord Roberts's despatch of September 10th, 1901, the following officers, non-commissioned officers, and men were mentioned for having performed special and meritorious service, viz. :—Colonel Charrington, Major B. T. Seckham, Captain and Adjutant E. A. Bulwer, Captain J. M. Steuart, and Major Guy Seckham (3rd North Stafford Regiment, attached 4th Battalion) ; Sergeant-Major W. Brown, Colour-Sergeant G. Payne, Sergeant Medlicot, Sergeant Beddowes, Lance-Sergeant Manison, and Private Donovan. Colonel Charrington was subsequently appointed a Companion of the Order of St. Michael and St. George, and Major B. T. Seckham a Companion of the Distinguished Service Order. These decorations were bestowed on them by the King at St. James's Palace. Sergeant-Major Brown and Colour-Sergeant Payne were awarded the Distinguished Service Medal, with which they were presented on 15th March, 1902, by Major-General Swaine, C.B., C.M.G., Commanding North-Western District.

In Lord Roberts's despatch of 17th June, 1902, Lieutenant and Quartermaster J. Penketh and Colour-Sergeant W. Hickey were also mentioned for special and meritorious service.

In Lord Kitchener's despatches of 29th July, 1902, Captain and Adjutant E. A. Bulwer, Lieutenant and Quartermaster J. Penketh, Sergeant-Instructor of Musketry H. Craddock, and Sergeant Bates were mentioned for special and meritorious service.

The following letters were received by Colonel Charrington from Lieutenant-General Lord Methuen, Commanding 1st Division, and Major-General Arthur Paget, Commanding 20th Brigade :—

DEAR COLONEL CHARRINGTON,—It is with great pleasure that I send you these few lines expressing my satisfaction with your fine Battalion. I knew from the manœuvres at Aldershot how well your men would march, and they did not belie their reputation. In discipline and in conduct on the "trek" from Boshoff to Lindley you had a fine opportunity of showing what you were all made of, and I felt perfect confidence in your men and officers alike. I always say, "Show me the Officers, and I will tell you the value of the Battalion." This remark applies in a favourable degree to your Battalion.

Yours sincerely,

(Signed) METHUEN.

Greysdorp, May 20th, 1901.

35, BELGRAVE SQUARE, S.W.

16th November, 1901.

MY DEAR COLONEL,—It will always be a source of regret to me, that I was not able to say a few parting words to you, your officers, non-commissioned officers, and men on the field for the gallant way in which they supported me during a very trying period of the campaign. As you remember, I only had 24 hours in which to entrain not only the prisoners and part of your Battalion to Cape Town, but the whole of the force to Pretoria, and I had not a moment to myself. I hope you will place on record my hearty appreciation of the gallant service rendered to 20th Brigade by the 4th South Staffordshire, notably at Lindley, and the subsequent operations at Bethlehem, ending in the capture of 4,000 of the enemy, of which your Battalion escorted 2,500 to Winberg, and, I believe, subsequently to Cape Town, without the loss of one prisoner.

My best thanks are also due to you for the cordial support you invariably gave me, and the excellent example set your men by the officers and non-commissioned officers no doubt contributed largely to the efficiency, good behaviour, and excellent marching of your Battalion whilst with me in South Africa.

Believe me,

Yours most sincerely,

(Signed) ARTHUR PAGET.

On Saturday, November 30th, 1901, Lord Dartmouth, Lord Lieutenant of the County, presented the South African War Medals to the Battalion in the Drill Hall, Walsall, which had been kindly lent for the occasion by Colonel Williamson, and which was elaborately decorated. Amongst those present were the Mayor of Walsall, Councillor Pearman-

87

Smith ; Colonel Williams, Commanding 38/64 Regimental
Districts ; Colonel Williamson, the Mayor and Ex-Mayor of
Lichfield, and many ladies. The officers of the Battalion
who were present were :—Colonel Charrington, C.M.G.,
Major Seckham, D.S.O., Captain Fitzwarine Smith, and
Captain and Adjutant Bulwer. The men of the Battalion
turned up voluntarily in good numbers, and 512 medals were
distributed. In opening the proceedings the Mayor extended
a cordial welcome to Lord Dartmouth, and to the 4th South
Staffordshire Regiment. At the conclusion of the presenta-
tion Colonel Charrington proposed a vote of thanks to the
Lord Lieutenant, and to Colonel Williamson for the use of the
Drill Hall. He read extracts from Lord Methuen's and
General Paget's letters, and in conclusion thanked Miss
Newman and the inhabitants of Walsall for the various com-
forts sent out by them to the Battalion whilst in Africa.
Colonel Williams seconded this vote, and Lord Dartmouth
replied, congratulating the Battalion on the services they had
rendered in South Africa, and for the manner in which they
had upheld the " prestige " of the old County. The proceedings concluded with hearty cheers for the King and Lord
Dartmouth.

The clasps gained by this Battalion were " Cape Colony "
and " Wittebergen," and this was the only Militia Battalion
which gained the latter clasp.   •

The strength of the Battalion on 31st December, 1901,
was :—Officers, 18 ; Warrant Officer, 1 ; Permanent Staff,
23 ; Non-commissioned Officers and Men, 1,054—Total
1,096.

PRINTED BY LOMAX'S SUCCESSORS, THE "JOHNSON'S HEAD," LICHFIELD.

Breinigsville, PA USA
29 January 2010
231635BV00003B/21/A